Tracing Your Ancestors

CHANCELLOR
PRESS

Acknowledgements

The publishers would like to thank Mrs Eileen Stage, Twickenham for sup-
plying the documents illustrated on pages 13, 14, 15 top and 15 bottom and
Simon Bargate, Twickenham for lending the Bible illustrated on page 10; the
illustrations on pages 23 bottom and 48 are reproduced by courtesy of Richmond Public Library; the Crown copyright records on pages 13, 14, 15
bottom, 17, 40, 41, 47, 49 are reproduced by permission of the Controller of
Her Majesty's Stationery Office; the map appearing on page 23 top is reproduced from the series covering parochial and probate boundaries for every
county by kind permission of the Trustees of the Institute of Heraldic and
Genealogical Studies © New Edition 1978; the photograph on page 46 appears
with the approval of the Keeper of the Records of Scotland; British Library,
London 60; The Church of Jesus Christ of Latter-Day Saints, Huddersfield
25; Hamlyn Group Picture Library 10, 28 left, 28 right, 34, 38, 44, 56;
Hamlyn Group – John Webb 20, 21 left, 21 right, 22 top, 22 bottom, 23
bottom, 48; Library of Congress, Prints & Photographs Division,
Washington 37; F G Tyack, Sheffield 6–7.

Cover photography:
Front; by kind permission of Mrs Mollie Sinclair; back; top left,
bottom left, bottom right by kind permission of Mrs Marjorie Revill
& Mrs Betty Brown; top right by kind permission of Mrs Mollie Sinclair;
bottom middle by kind permission of Mr Brian Revill.

First published in Great Britain in 1982 by Hamlyn, a division of
Octopus Publishing Group

Published in 1987 by Treasure Press
Reprinted 1989, 1990, 1991,1992, 1993, 1994, 1995, 1997, 1998

This 2002 edition published by Chancellor Press, an imprint of
Bounty Books, a division of Octopus Publishing Group Ltd,
2–4 Heron Quays, London E14 4JP

ISBN 0 7537 0678 4

Printed and bound in China

Contents

Introduction

Genealogy, or the study of pedigrees, is not quite the same thing as family history. The genealogist is strictly concerned with establishing family relationships and descent, and 'history', in the fullest sense, is largely incidental. The family historian is concerned with much more than establishing that Great-Grandfather Field was a coal merchant who was born in Huddersfield in 1852, married there in 1878 and died in Sheffield in 1916. He wants to find out as much as possible about his subject. After establishing the basic genealogical facts, he will probably go on to study books on the coal-retailing business and life in Victorian Huddersfield. Family history can and does make an important contribution to history generally. These days, the emphasis in history is less on the careers of kings, the tactics of battles or the details of treaties and much more on the lives of ordinary people. Most schools teach a course on the history of their own district, whilst virtually every little village and suburb has its own local historian, maybe even its own printed local history. Family history can often be linked with studies of this sort.

Of course, genealogy is also history; in fact, it is arguably the oldest form of history we have. One need look no further than the Book of Genesis to see what a vital part family history played in early human societies. In many societies, power and property depended on inheritance, and thus it was important to remember who your grandfather was, who his father was, and so on. Indeed, this is still one of the *raisons d'être* of genealogy: it is not unusual for family quarrels to occur over wills, for example, as a result of confusion over family relationships.

There are many reasons why people should wish to trace their ancestors. As a rule, there is no practical motive at work; it is simply a matter of interest for most people to know how they came to be who they are. There is not necessarily any snobbery involved, although it must be admitted that this has often been a major element. Middle-class Victorians were desperately keen to believe they had Norman ancestors, while in New England today there still seem to be a remarkably large number of white Anglo-Saxon ladies who had an ancestor on the *Mayflower*. There is, it appears, a particular compulsion to trace one's ancestors if they were comparatively recent immigrants to the country. One often finds that societies who, through racial, religious or other reasons, are distinct from the majority of the population are especially interested in their genealogy. The descendants of European settlers in North America, Australia and other countries overseas are often more concerned with their roots than people whose ancestors have presumably lived in Britain for many centuries.

Often the search is set in motion by some long-repeated but unsupported family legend that they come from noble blood or had great estates, or when, by an odd coincidence during a conversation between strangers, a chance remark reveals that they are distantly related. Everybody has far more relatives than he or she knows personally: family circles seldom extend much beyond first or second cousins, if that. In fact most of the people whose families have been settled in the same country for many hundreds of years are probably remotely related to each other. This is the result of the way in which ancestors multiply as the generations march backwards in time. A complete family tree resembles an inverted pyramid, with you as the sharp point at the bottom. The next generation contains two people (your parents), the next four (your grandparents), the next eight (great-grandparents) and the next sixteen. All this – five generations – is quite manageable, but go back another six generations and your direct ancestors, doubling in each generation, have reached the unaccommodating number of 1,024 (assuming there are no marriages between cousins, which cuts down the number). In twenty generations the number has grown to over half a million; if you go back a generation or two further than that, which takes you to about the 14th century, you find that the number of your ancestors exceeds the total contemporary population of England! Naturally, this does not mean that every English person today is related to all the rest, since the ancestors of a great many of the current population came from some other country at some time since the 14th century. It is probably quite rare to find a family that goes back for more than a few generations without foreign blood coming in somewhere. In any case, this whole exercise is really academic: after all, if you take the Bible literally, we are all descended from Adam and Eve. But one important point arising out of the pyramidal effect of the generations is that it does offer a very wide choice as to which line of forbears you pursue. Genealogy is primarily concerned with descent through the male line – son, father, grandfather, etc. – but there is very little reason why anyone who has a general interest in his forbears should pursue this line to the exclusion of others. Your mother's family may be much more fascinating! People are usually interested in their own family name, or surname, but it seems a pity to be bound by the somewhat arbitrary convention that, in England, wives have customarily taken their husband's name on marriage.

It is really out of the question to establish *all* your ancestors at a greater distance than five or six generations: it becomes much too complicated. However, when you embark on your genealogical research, you should make a note of all significant information, not just the facts affecting the particular line you are following. Other branches may become interesting later, and you will then regret that you did not pay attention to them in the first place, thus saving yourself from having to cover the same ground twice. If you are setting out to prove or disprove that your Great-Aunt Emily was correct in her insistence that some famous historical figure is one of your ancestors, you may be compelled to follow an unorthodox line. The late Canon W. E. Sims of Liverpool was intrigued by the legend in his wife's family that Oliver Cromwell was among their ancestors, which, on the face of it, could not be true as Cromwell had no known direct descendants. However, he set out to trace his wife's pedigree and eventually found that she was descended from Cromwell's sister, so the legend was not without substance.

If you merely wish to find out as much about your forbears as you can, you will probably be forced to discard some lines of descent fairly soon through lack of evidence. It would be foolish to pretend that anyone can, with sufficient perseverance, trace his or her family back to the time of the Norman Conquest. Only a few people can, and it is seldom by direct descent in the male line. It is also assumed that titled families possess an ancient heritage that goes back to the Normans, if not to the Anglo-Saxons, and that the higher the rank of nobility the more ancient the lineage. This is far from the truth. Most titled families were commoners in the not-too-distant past. Dukes are especially suspect as a significant proportion of them are descended from illegitimate children of Charles II. The oldest English ducal family (the title was originally reserved for royal princes) is that of the Howards of Norfolk; their dukedom dates only from the late 15th century whilst the earliest Howard ancestor of whom one can feel reasonably certain was a judge who died about 1308. Earls and certain country gentry are more respectable, genealogically speaking, than dukes. However, as patriotic historians are fond of asserting, there has always been a relatively greater degree of social mobility in England than in most other European countries, so there is always a chance that you will discover ancestral connections with the nobility or landed gentry. If you do, the genealogical search becomes much easier. If you do not, you will probably not be able to trace your family as far back as you may have hoped, certainly not to the Normans and probably not to the Middle Ages.

How far, then, can you expect to go? Obviously, that is a question which cannot be answered exactly because success depends largely on luck – not to mention time, money and determination. However, in general there is a very good chance of tracing your ancestors, no matter how humble, to the late 18th century. This is simply because the necessary documentary evidence is likely to extend approximately that far. Documentary records are, on the whole, better preserved in England because the country has suffered relatively few major domestic upheavals in the past five hundred years. Luck becomes an increasingly important element the farther back you go, but once you have returned to a period before the Industrial Revolution certain advantages begin to work in your favour, partly compensating for the more patchy character of the records. In particular, people tended to move about less than they have done more recently.

Following page. Fine example of a family tree compiled by an amateur family historian, Francis George Tyack. It is particularly good in its use of family photographs; Mr Tyack is in the group portrait on the left of the family tree.

PED 3
A1 SIZE

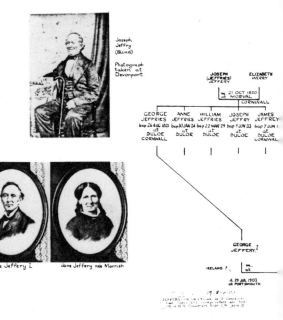

Joseph Jeffry (Blind) Photograph taken at Devonport

JOSEPH (JEFFRIES) JEFFERY — ELIZABETH WERRY
m. 21 OCT 1820 at MORVAL, CORNWALL

GEORGE JEFFRIES bap 26 AUG 1821 at DULOE CORNWALL | ANNE JEFFRIES bap 30 JAN 24 at DULOE | WILLIAM JEFFRIES bap 22 MAR 29 at DULOE | JOSEPH JEFFRY bap 9 JUN 33 at MORVAL | JAMES JEFFREY bap 7 JUN 1 at DULOE CORNWALL

George Jeffery I   Jane Jeffery née Morrish

GEORGE JEFFERY I
IRELAND ? — m.
d. 29 JUL 1903 at PORTSMOUTH

JEFFERY... 29 8...
A WIDOWER 22 YEARS

RYDE, EAST PARISH OF ST HELENS ECCLESIASTICAL DISTRICT OF ST JOHNS SEAVIEW MORRAL HOUSE			1871 CENSUS PUBLIC RECORD OFFICE REF RG 10 1166	
NAME AND SURNAME		AGE	RANK, PROFESSION, OR OCCUPATION	WHERE BORN
GEORGE JEFFERY	HEAD	49	CHIEF OFFICER OF COAST GUARD ACTIVE LIST	CORNWALL ~ DULOE
JANE	do WIFE	49		CORNWALL ~ REDRUTH
ANNIE	do DAU	22	PRINTER	IRELAND
JOHN	do SON	15		DAVENPORT ←(No?)
THOMAS	do SON	13	SCHOLAR	IRELAND
JANE	do DAU	10	SCHOLAR	IRELAND
ROBERT	do SON	8	SCHOLAR	IRELAND

IRELAND

Anyone who has to make inquiries into records in the Republic of Ireland must face the fact that in a civil war (after the connection with Britain had been broken) many of the records of Ireland were destroyed. This happened because the Irish Republicans had their own quarrels, and on April 13, 1921, the Public Record Office in Dublin was occupied by armed men, and on June 30, 1921, the portion of the Office in which the records were kept was destroyed. Vast quantities of records which are used by genealogists were thus lost. For example, out of the collection of wills, only eleven wills of the Prerogative Court and one diocesan will were saved.* Of the parish registers, 817 were burned. These registers were those of the (Protestant) Church of Ireland, which was disestablished in 1869.

PAGES 106-7 IN "YOUR FAMILY TREE"
BY L.G. PINE
HERBERT JENKINS, 1961

BORN IN IRELAND

JOSEPH JEFFERY d. at aged 32 | JOHN JEFFERY I d. in infancy | JAMES JEFFERY d. in infancy

SEE PED 2 & PED 14 TYACK

RYDE, ISLE OF WIGHT

On Wednesday last a wedding took place at Trinity Church, when Samuel J. Tyack, esq., of Chacewater, Cornwall, nephew of J. Tyack, esq., of Salem House, Chacewater, was united to Miss Ann Jeffery, eldest daughter of Mr. G. Jeffery, chief officer of the Coastguard.

FROM FAMILY BIBLE

ANNIE JEFFERY b. 15 FEB 1849 at ISLAND MAGEE, IRELAND m. 30 OCT 1872 at RYDE d. 21 JUN 1933 at RYDE

SAMUEL JOSEPH TYACK b. 16 MAR 1844 at MORRO VELHO, BRAZIL d. 29 MAY 1926 at RYDE

BORN AT PADSTOW, CORNWALL (ST COLUMB MAJOR)   BORN AT PORTSMOUTH, HAMPSHIRE

FREDERICK GEORGE TYACK b. 1873 d. 1874 | JANE LOUISA TYACK b. 1874 d. 1893 | JOHN EDWIN TYACK b. 10 JAN 1877 | SAMUEL JOSEPH II TYACK b. 20 SEP 1878 at KINGSTON, PORTSEA ISLAND | ERNEST TYACK b. 1880 d. 1881 | ANNIE TYACK b. 2 JAN 1885

SAMUEL JOSEPH TYACK I, WITH HIS WIFE ANNIE AND THEIR THREE SURVIVING CHILDREN, WENT TO BRAZIL ABOUT 1891. ANNIE AND THE CHILDREN RETURNED TO BRITAIN ABOUT JUNE 1894 (THIS DATE SUGGESTED BY SAMUEL JOSEPH II'S TESTIMONIAL FROM BRAZIL AND JOHN EDWIN'S APPLICATION TO JOIN THE ROYAL NAVY).

SEE PED 4 BARTLE & HIGGS

ANNIE TYACK WENT TO VANCOUVER, CANADA, IN 19.. SHE RETURNED TO RYDE IN 19..
d. 27 JAN 1965 at NEWPORT, I.o.W.
BURIED IN SAME GRAVE AS HER FATHER AND MOTHER AT RYDE, ISLE OF WIGHT

JOHN EDWIN TYACK m. 3 APR 1905 at PORTSEA d. 25 OCT 1969 at PORTCHESTER A WIDOWER 21 YEARS

EMILY ROSE MARIE REEDS b. 1880 d. 13 JUN 1948 at PORTCHESTER

SAMUEL JOSEPH TYACK m. 22 SEP 1906 at BOGNOR, SUSSEX d. 22 FEB 1924 at WANDSWORTH LONDON

ALICE EMILY BARTLE b. 15 MAY 1880 at STRATFORD, LONDON d. 25 MAR 1966 at SHEFFIELD A WIDOW 42 YEARS

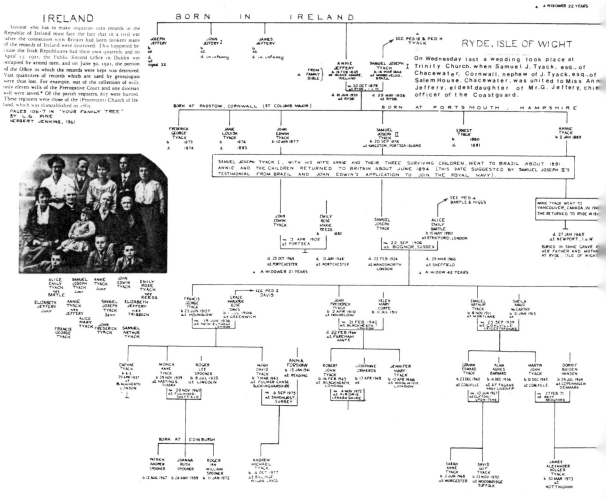

ALICE EMILY TYACK née BARTLE | SAMUEL JOSEPH TYACK Junr | ANNIE TYACK Junr | JOHN EDWIN TYACK

ELIZABETH JEFFERY Junr | ANNIE TYACK née JEFFERY | SAMUEL JOSEPH TYACK Senr | ELIZABETH JEFFERY née TRIBBECK | EMILY ROSE TYACK née REEDS

ALICE MARY TYACK | JOHN FREDERICK TYACK

FRANCIS GEORGE TYACK | SAMUEL ARTHUR TYACK

FRANCIS GEORGE TYACK b. 23 JUN 1907 at HOUNSLOW m. 19 JUN 1936 at NEW ELTHAM, LONDON | GRACE MARJORIE ROSE DAVIS b. 2 APR 1906 at GREENWICH

SEE PED 2 DAVIS

HUGH DAVID TYACK b. 7 MAR 1943 at FULMER CHASE BUCKINGHAMSHIRE | ANNA FORSHAW b. ... at READING m. 6 SEP 1975 at SANDHURST, SURREY

JOHN FREDERICK TYACK b. 15 JAN 1941 at HOUNSLOW m. 21 FEB 1942 at BLACKHEATH LONDON d. 22 FEB 1966 at FAREHAM HANTS | HELEN MARY COFFE b. 31 JUL 1911

SAMUEL ARTHUR TYACK b. 8 NOV 1911 at MORTLAKE m. 23 SEP 1939 at COALVILLE LEICESTERSHIRE | SHEILA MAUD McCARTHY b. 31 JAN 1913

DAPHNE TYACK b. 29 APR 1937 at BLACKHEATH LONDON | MONICA ANNE TYACK b. 23 JUN 1939 at LINCOLN m. 29 NOV 1965 at SHEFFIELD | ROGER LEE SPOONER b. 8 JUL 1935

ROBERT JOHN TYACK b. 16 FEB 1943 at BLACKHEATH LONDON | JOSEPHINE ORMEROD b. 17 APR 1948 m. 4 NOV 1972 at AIRDRIE, LANARKSHIRE | JENNIFER MARY TYACK b. 10 APR 1946 at WOOLWICH LONDON

GILLIAN EDWARD TYACK b. 23 DEC 1960 at COALVILLE m. 10 JUN 1967 at CLIFTON-UPON-TEME | ALMA AGNES BARNARD b. 14 DEC 1936 at ST FAGANS nr CARDIFF | MARTIN JOHN TYACK b. 31 DEC 1945 at COALVILLE | DORRIT BOISEN HANSEN b. 29 JUL 1949 at COPENHAGEN DENMARK m. 27 FEB 71 at WEST BRIDGFORD

BORN AT EDINBURGH

PATRICK ANDREW SPOONER b. 12 AUG 1967 at WORCESTER | JOANNA RUTH SPOONER b. 24 MAY 1969 | ROGER IAN WILLIAM SPOONER b. 11 JAN 1972

ANDREW MICHAEL TYACK b. 4 OCT 1977 at BILLINGE WIGAN, LANCS

SARAH ANNE TYACK b. 3 JUN 1968 at WORCESTER | DAVID GUY TYACK b. 23 NOV 1970 at WOODBRIDGE SUFFOLK

JAMES ALEXANDER HOLGER TYACK b. 30 MAR 1973 at NOTTINGHAM

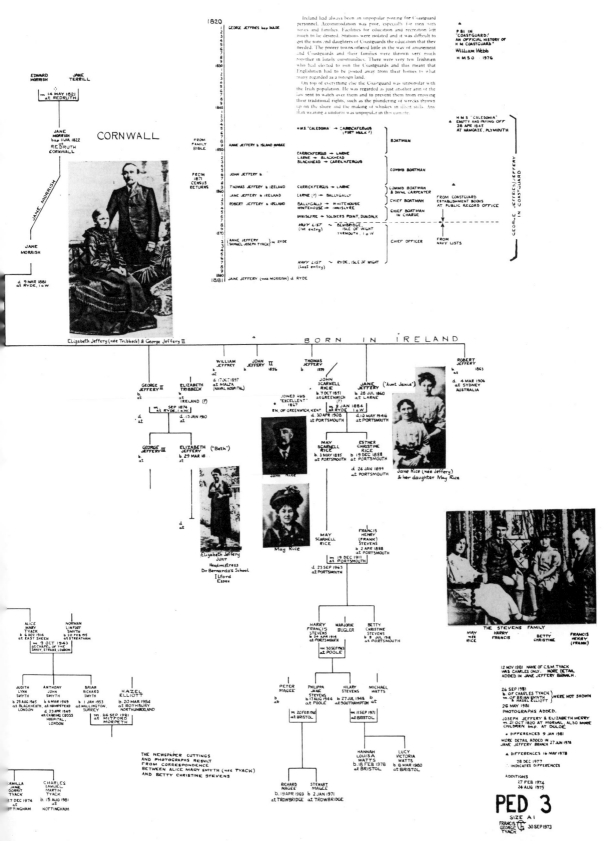

Modern research has in fact shown that the population of England was more mobile in the past than has usually been assumed: few families have actually remained in the same village for centuries, unless anchored there by the possession of land in the district. But, although they were seldom stationary for long, families generally did not move very far. When they disappear from one parish they are frequently to be rediscovered, a generation earlier, in an adjacent one.

If you manage to trace your ancestors to the second half of the 18th century, there is a fair chance of tracing them back another hundred years, to the reign of Charles II. His reign was preceded by the Civil War and Commonwealth, the time of greatest administrative turmoil since the Middle Ages. During this period, for example, parish records, the chief genealogical sources for that time, were disrupted and in many cases lost. You should, therefore, feel that if you succeed in tracing your ancestors to the second half of the 17th century you will have done very well. Anything further is an unexpected bonus. If you are fortunate, parish registers may take you back to the reign of Henry VIII, but you are very unlikely to make further progress unless you belong to an old titled or landowning family.

Clearly, if you are an orphan from Liverpool named Murphy, your chances of locating your forbears are less good than if your name is Hetherington-Foxways and you have inherited ancient family estates in the Home Counties. Possession of an unusual surname is an undoubted advantage although, as we shall see, it can sometimes be a source of confusion. However, you should never allow either a common surname or a paucity of information about your most recent forbears to put you off the search before you begin.

Having an unusual name is, in fact, often the decisive factor which impels an individual to make a search for his ancestors. The assumption is made, not always correctly, that uncommon names will be easier to trace than names like Smith, Jones or Robinson. This was certainly one of the motives that prompted Gordon Honeycombe, the well-known writer and broadcaster, to undertake the search for his ancestors which became the basis for a popular television series on the subject. Those programmes no doubt encouraged many other people to embark on a search they had hitherto only contemplated, if at all, as a vague project for the future. The book published in conjunction with the television series, *Discovering Your Family History* by Don Steel, is well worth reading because it combines sound general guidance with Gordon Honeycombe's particularly interesting 'case history', as typical as any history of a single family could be expected to be.

Starting Off

Before you start the investigation of your family's history, the first thing to do is to make sure that someone has not written it already. It may seem unlikely that there is a printed history of your family that you have never heard of, but many hundreds have been published. Moreover, as your search proceeds, you may find a connection by marriage with a family whose history has been written but which did not appear to have any relevance to your own work initially. Besides printed works, there may be a manuscript history or pedigree, which can be harder to locate; there may even be some kind of genealogical record worked out by an earlier member of the family. This will need checking, but at least it gives you a good basis to start from. It is very annoying to spend weeks trying to find out the name of your great-grandfather only to discover the answer already existed in a family document of which you were not aware. For printed records of families, you should consult one of the genealogical guides (see bibliography). Manuscripts are less easy to trace but the best place to inquire in England is the Society of Genealogists, who will be able to advise you of any catalogued genealogical manuscripts. You can also check the catalogue of the British Library, in which (fortunately) family histories are entered under the name of the family as well as the author.

The next step is to assemble all the available evidence you can from private sources, including, of course, your own. It would be a stroke of luck to find that someone has already compiled a family tree or written an account of the family at some earlier period, but there will almost certainly be documents of some kind – certificates of birth or marriage, old letters, diaries, bills and receipts, and so on. At this stage you want to know as much as possible about the lives of your immediate predecessors; almost anything may be useful so do not be too discriminating.

Many families possess an old family bible. This was a traditional wedding present for brides, in which the details of her marriage and the birth of her children were later recorded. This may give you several generations of your ancestors at a single stroke and it should be comparatively easy to check the information later against certified documents.

The family bible and other documents may not be in the possession of your immediate family. An old bible may have passed to another branch of the family several generations earlier and still be available although unknown to you. Some people tend to hoard old documents, others to throw them away at the first opportunity. With any luck, there should be at least one hoarder in your family. You should therefore contact all your relatives, including those you have never met, to find out whether they possess any documents or other family memorabilia which may prove informative. At the same time you can ask them whether they have any personal memories, ideas or notions about the family that may provide clues for further research. It is no good writing to your second cousin twice removed, who perhaps lives in another country, with a vague request for information about the family. It is better to make up a questionnaire, copies of which can be circulated to all known members of the family, leaving space for 'any other information' such as family legends and traditions. Older relatives are, obviously, of particular interest. How often one hears people say, too late: 'If only I had asked Aunt So-and-So!'

Detectives in criminal cases are always telling witnesses that they wish to hear *all* the facts, not just those that seem relevant to the witness. This is a sound basis for all research, including genealogical research which is itself a detective hunt of a kind. A tit-bit of gossip that means nothing when first heard may, once more facts have been learned, prove to be significant. Equally, of course, it may

Arthur Freer Bargate born Feb 11th 1866.

Lawrence Heath Bargate born August 6th 1890.

Phyllis Adaline Bargate born July 29th 1891
both born at 32 Park Hall Rd, East Finchley N.

Cecil Vincent Bargate. born 20th Dec: 1901
Ronald Arthur Bargate. born 8th Sept: 1906
Geoffrey Norman Bargate born 3rd March: 1908
Marjorie Kate Bargate. born 5th Sept: 1912
Kenneth Alfred Bargate born 16th Feb: 1914.

The family bible is particularly useful as a possible source of genealogical information. Here four generations of the Bargate family are recorded on the fly leaf.

not, but at this stage no stone should be left unturned.

Relatives may be especially useful if they happen to live in the district from which your family comes, while your own branch of the family has perhaps emigrated to another country. He or she may even turn out to be willing to carry out some on-the-spot research of a simple kind which you cannot easily do, such as checking the tombstones in the local churchyard or inspecting the parish registers.

Besides actual documents, there are many other possible sources of information among old family possessions. An important clue in one case was provided by a silver teapot of unusual design. It could be assigned to a firm of Regency silversmiths whose records survived. They revealed for whom the teapot was made, and the customer concerned turned out to be a vital missing link in the family tree.

Family heirlooms and the stories connected with them may often indicate avenues to be explored, regardless of any direct evidence they may supply. At the least they suggest whether or not the family was a wealthy one. A family of farm labourers is unlikely to have had a silver teapot, although a family of cabinetmakers may well have passed on some fine furniture.

Photographs and paintings can often provide more information than may at first appear. The style or technique makes it possible to date them fairly accurately, and greater precision may be offered by what appears in the background. It may be possible to identify some article of furniture still in the family; clothes are also a good guide to date and to social status. For example, an old photograph which turned up in one family showed a group of men in frock coats outside a railway station, apparently forming a reception party. On the basis of the clothes and a motor car in the background, the date could be assigned to about the year 1920. The railway station gave the location, and a search among local newspaper files revealed that the town concerned had received a royal visit in March 1921. The newspaper also listed the names of the people presented to the royal visitor, and they included the grandfather of the owner of the photograph. Since the date and time of the arrival of the royal train were also given, it was possible to deduce the hour, almost the minute, at which the photograph had been taken.

Whenever possible, it is advisable to obtain the actual documents or photocopies of them. Other information should be carefully noted, probably in a loose-leaf notebook so that pages can be added in the appropriate place when more facts are discovered. On the basis of this family information, it will be possible to make a beginning on your family tree, for you will be unlucky if you cannot trace three or four generations from these sources. Probably some of your information relies on hearsay rather than documentary evidence. If your purpose in tracing your ancestors is to prove legally that you are descended from a certain person, you will eventually have to secure proper documentary proof of the apparent facts you have learned. To what extent you do that may depend largely on how serious your researches are. If your mother tells you your great-grandfather's name was Eric, she is almost certainly correct, but of course her assurance is not legal proof. For that you would need, ideally, a copy of your great-grandfather's birth certificate, or some similar form of corroboration. If you are only pursuing your investigation out of a sense of curiosity, you may decide to seek no further evidence. However, a professional genealogist takes nothing on trust; for example, he does not assume that 'facts' reported in a newspaper report are correct (in *some* respects they are almost always not). All evidence needs corroboration, and amateur genealogists frequently – sometimes, no doubt, without ever becoming aware of it – make a complete hash of their pedigree by assuming that what is probable is actually true. The golden rule is *doublecheck everything*. If you make a mistake with family relationships a couple of generations back by assuming – this can happen quite easily – that two people of opposite sex sharing the same premises and the same surname are man and wife, your whole family tree from that point backwards is thrown into error. They may happen to have been brother and sister.

When you are certain that you have assembled all the information you can reasonably expect to obtain from family and local sources, you will have to make several important decisions. First, are you going to carry on with the task yourself, or are you going to employ professional assistance? It is of course possible to hire a professional genealogist who, on the basis of the information you can provide, will take over from this point. He or she will probably work faster than you can, if only because of familiarity with the main sources and procedures involved. But such a course will involve you in considerable expense, besides depriving you of much of the fun. Moreover, no matter how conscientious your researcher is, he will not have a personal interest in the task. It is therefore better, on the whole, to do the job yourself as far as you can. If you happen to live on the other side of the world from the country in which most of your research must take place, then obviously your opportunity to conduct a personal search will be limited. Nevertheless, it is surprising how much can be accomplished by mail or in a visit of a couple of weeks, if you are well prepared. You may find that the best alternative is to combine the two procedures by doing as much as you can yourself whilst employing professional help when necessary. Any amateur genealogist is, in fact, likely to need professional help at some stage, but it is often possible to complete a long and complicated piece of genealogical research entirely by mail, and at no substantially greater cost than would be incurred if you were on the spot. For example, it costs less to obtain a copy of a birth certificate from the General Register Office in London if you go there in person, but unless you happen to be in London anyway, the extra charge is less than the cost of a special journey. If you are visiting Britain from overseas, your time will be limited, and you will not want to waste it in making preliminary inquiries which could have been completed before your arrival.

Before you start on serious genealogical research in large record offices and other institutions, you should make yourself familiar with some of the problems you are likely to to encounter. If you have never done any original research before, you will find it bewildering and frustrating if you start 'cold'. It may be worth your while becoming a member of the Society of Genealogists in London, which entitles you to a free copy of their quarterly magazine and the use of the library (available to non-members for a fee). The Society may sometimes undertake to do some research on your behalf, and this is less expensive if you are a member (but it is still fairly costly and should if possible be confined to fairly straightforward inquiries which can be completed in an hour or two). If you have decided to hire a researcher for a longer project, you can approach the Association of Genealogists and Record Agents in London, who will furnish a list of capable people and the areas in which they specialise. It is unwise to succumb to the invitations of agencies who advertise in the press, promising to discover your family's pedigree and coat of arms. Some are perfectly legitimate, but there are rogues in this business as in others.

There is a large and growing number of local and family history societies in Britain. If you know the district you are interested in, you should certainly get in touch with the local society. Even if you do not get concrete help from this source, you will at least get encouragement and advice, which at this stage are important. Local family history societies can also give valuable guidance, for instance, in pointing out obscure printed works relevant to your research which you might otherwise have missed. The addresses of local societies can be obtained from the Federation of Family History Societies which keeps records of all its members' publications and publishes a regular newsletter of their activities. Join a family history class at your nearest adult education centre. If there isn't one, then write to your local education department and ask them to provide one.

Helpful institutions in Ireland are the Genealogical Office in Dublin and the Ulster Historical Foundation in Belfast which, if you send as many details as you can of your ancestors' Ulster origins, will undertake a search for a reasonable fee. In Scotland, the Scots Ancestry Research Society in Edinburgh performs a similar function. It is, however, always advisable to ask for an estimate of the cost of a search by one of these bodies, or indeed from any other institution or individual whose assistance you may employ.

Births, Marriages and Deaths

Once you have acquired all the material you can from printed sources, local libraries, private information from relatives, etc., you are ready to embark upon outside research in official archives.

Before you begin, make sure all your data are accurately and clearly recorded. There is no golden rule about how you assemble your material, but it is advisable to use loose-leaf notebooks and/or index cards, which will allow new information to be added in the correct place without causing confusion. You will probably have drawn up a family tree (for alternative ways of doing this, consult some of the printed family histories), with separate cards or sheets of paper for each individual who appears on it. It is better to record biographical details separately from the family tree, as the latter will otherwise soon become an impenetrable muddle. There you need only record full name, date of birth, perhaps occupation, marriage and date of death. Very likely you will find you have to include two or more ancestors with the same name. Be sure you prevent future mistakes by numbering or otherwise identifying them clearly – by occupation, for example. One keen amateur genealogist, whose ancestors adopted a confusingly small number of first names, used invariably to refer to them in conversation as 'John Kennet shoemaker' or 'John Kennet carpenter', in a manner similar to that encountered in Welsh villages where many people share the same surname – 'Jones the Milk', 'Jones the Post', etc.

All births, marriages and deaths are officially recorded, but the system of civil registration is comparatively recent. In England and Wales it began in 1837, in Scotland in 1855, and in Ireland not until 1864.

There are district registries in every county in England, and if you are quite certain of the area in which your ancestors lived, you can approach the district registry office for the documents you want.

However, even then you may be disappointed since births or deaths do not always take place in the home district. Otherwise, it is necessary to apply to the General Register Office, St Catherine's House, London. Copies of all birth, marriage and death certificates can be obtained by post, providing you can furnish adequate facts: ideally, for a birth certificate, full name and date of birth plus names of parents. However, it is best not to list the father's occupation as it was not uncommon for a man to change his job frequently. It is perhaps unlikely that all these details are known, in which case give as many as you can; similarly with marriage or death certificates. The staff will undertake a search requested by post, but they are naturally reluctant to cover a very long period, especially for a common name. If you have, for example, only the name and a very rough estimate of the date, then you or someone working on your behalf will have to search the indexes in person.

Archivists and researchers are generally thought of as frail, dusty people with poor eyesight but a few days research in the General Register Office (GRO) can in fact be recommended as vigorous exercise. The indexes are extremely large – the earlier ones weigh over 20 lbs each – and constantly carrying them back and forth between shelf and table (there is no seating) can be very exhausting. It can also be rather depressing, since at first you are likely to feel like someone searching for a needle in a haystack. Success, however, will put new life into you.

The amount of research you will have to do depends on how much information you have to start with, so do make sure you have *all* the available data before you begin. If you want the birth certificate of an ancestor whose name and date of birth you know, then you should run him or her down fairly quickly, though you may have to consult four or five volumes of the index, since they

GIVEN AT THE GENERAL REGISTER OFFICE,
SOMERSET HOUSE, LONDON

Application Number *775/4*

REGISTRATION DISTRICT	*Bideford*								
BIRTH in the Sub-district of	*Parkham*			in the	*County of Devon*				
Columns:— 1	2	3	4	5	6	7	8	9	10*
No.	When and where born	Name, if any	Sex	Name, and surname of father	Name, surname, and maiden surname of mother	Occupation of father	Signature, description, and residence of informant	When registered	Signature of registrar	Name entered after registration

CERTIFIED to be a true copy of an entry in the certified copy of a Register of Births in the District above mentioned.
Given at the GENERAL REGISTER OFFICE, SOMERSET HOUSE, LONDON, under the Seal of the said Office, the *24th* day of *April* 19 *72*.

See note overleaf

BX 679779

Certified copy of a birth certificate, from the General Record Office, which records place and date of birth, names of parents, father's occupation, and identifies the person giving the information (usually a parent). In this case it records the birth of a daughter to Henry and Sarah Crang in 1844.

are arranged by quarter years. As the GRO records the *registration* of birth, and you know only the year, you may find the entry in the volume after the one you expect. For instance, a birth at Christmas 1880 was probably not registered until January 1881. A problem sometimes encountered at this stage is that several people are found with exactly the same name and approximate date of birth as the ancestor you are looking for.

Having filled in the relevant details from the index on the form provided and given the form to the official on duty, you will in due course receive a copy of the birth certificate. Note that certificates cannot be obtained on the spot, which is another reason in favour of working by mail if possible. The certificate will probably give you some facts you did not know before regardless of the birth of the person concerned. If we assume, for the sake of argument, that the ancestor whose birth certificate you now hold is the earliest of whom you had any knowledge, you now know who his or her parents were! The birth certificate should state the full names of both, plus the mother's maiden name, the father's occupation, the place of birth, and the name and address of the person who provided the information, usually a parent.

The next step is to look for the marriage of the parents, having obtained their names from the birth certificate. Start working from the quarter that the child was born and continue backwards. Don't forget that women in Victorian times contin-

ued to have children over a twenty year period or so; if the birth you have found is that of the last child, then you can have a long hunt backwards. If you still cannot find the marriage, then try working forwards from the date of the child's birth, again remembering that it may not have occurred after the birth of the child or subsequent children or even not at all.

Having found the entry for the man you suppose to be the husband, you can check the wife's entry under her maiden name in the same quarter of the index, although it may not be in the same volume as her husband's as there are a number of these in the earlier years to cover the full alphabet. If the reference number is the same for both parties, then you have the correct marriage. If not, then start hunting again. If you do not have the maiden surname of the wife, then you cannot double check in this way. Sometimes it is quicker to search in the indexes for the wife's maiden name first if she has a more uncommon name than her husband.

When you get the marriage certificate, it will tell you the date and place of the marriage, the name of the husband, his marital status (i.e. bachelor or widower), his age, his occupation, his address and also the name and occupation of his father. For the wife, it will give similar information except her occupation is very rarely listed, even when it is known she had one. Unfortunately, the names of the mothers of the partners is not given. Occasionally it will mention that the father is deceased. If this is not stated, it does not necessarily mean that the father is still alive at the time the marriage certificate was issued.

Many of the early marriages only give the age of the partners as 'of full age' therefore you only know that they are allegedly 'over 21'. If this is the case, then you are unable to work out when they were born. Often the wife was older than the husband

Application Number ... 3937 D.

Registration District ... Bideford

1854. Marriage solemnized at in the Parish Church
in the Parish of Bideford   in the county of Devon

No.	When married	Name and Surname	Age	Condition	Rank or profession	Residence at the time of marriage	Father's name and surname	Rank or profession of father
66	March 25th	Henry Crang / Sarah Bowden	full age / full age	Bachelor / Widow	Farmer / ---	Monk Leigh / Bideford	James Crang / John Gorman	Farmer / Thatcher

Married in the Parish Church according to the rites and ceremonies of the Established Church by Banns by me William Walter, Rector

This marriage was solemnized between us, { Henry Crang / Sarah Bowden } in the presence of us, { Henry Crang / Wm J. Blight }

CERTIFIED to be a true copy of an entry in the certified copy of a Register of Marriages in the District above mentioned.
Given at the GENERAL REGISTER OFFICE, LONDON, under the Seal of the said Office, the 6th day of February 1980.

MB 222281

This certificate is issued in pursuance of section 65 of the Marriage Act 1949. Subsection (3) of that section provides that any certified copy of an entry purporting to be sealed or stamped with the seal of the General Register Office shall be received as evidence of the marriage to which it relates without any further or other proof of the entry, and no certified copy purporting to have been given in the said Office shall be of any force or effect unless it is sealed or stamped as aforesaid.

CAUTION—Any person who (1) falsifies any of the particulars on this certificate, or (2) uses a falsified certificate as true, knowing it to be false, is liable to prosecution.

Henry Crang's marriage certificate shows that his wife Sarah was a widow and her maiden name was Gorman whereas it was recorded on their daughter Thomazin's birth certificate as Bowden. Both parties described themselves as 'of full age'; not until both death certificates were obtained was it known that Sarah was 13 years older than her husband.

and this does not make itself known until the death certificates are obtained.

The marriage certificate will also tell you whether the couple were married in the established church (i.e. Church of England), a Non-Conformist chapel, Roman Catholic Church Jewish Synagogue or Registry Office. If they were married in the Church of England, then it will state whether it was by banns read in the church or by licence. Do not be surprised if both parties give the same adress. Sometimes this way done to save having the banns read in both parishes and thus saving money, or was an address of convenience to allow them to marry after four weeks' residence in another area than their own, possibly due to their parents disagreeing to the marriage.

If neither party could sign their name, then they would have to make a mark at the bottom of the certificate as would the two witnesses. The names of the latter can be important for they were often relations of the couple, thus further names can be added to the family tree.

Death certificates are rather less informative. When searching for a death before 1866, no age is given in the index therefore it is not possible to decide if the death is that of a young or old person. The death certificate itself gives the date and place of death, the name, age and occupation of the person, cause of death, signature, description and residence of the informant and when the death was

registered. The death and place of death can sometimes be discovered in the index of wills at Somerset House if the individual had made a will or there were letters of administration for probate of his estate. However, vital pieces of information can be undiscovered if you do not get a copy of the death certificate (see copy of death certificate illustrated above).

Sometimes the death certificate will reveal the fact that the person had died away from his own home, possibly at the house of a son or daughter, who then had registered the death; more information for the family tree. Again beware of the age given especially if a neighbour had to register the death.

Exceptional difficulties may arise in certain cases. For instance, this may occur in the case of an adopted or illegitimate child, in a change of name after a birth was registered, or occasionally in the simple failure of parents to register the birth at all.

It is wise to remember, moreover, that the details given in birth and marriage certificates may not always be accurate. It is not unknown for a bride to give her age as somewhat less than it really is! Sooner or later in your research, you are almost certain to come across discrepancies of this sort. Make careful note of them and, with luck, the solution will eventually appear as your work progresses.

In Ireland, the equivalent institutions are the GRO in Dublin and the GRO in Belfast (since 1922). In Scotland, the actual registers of births, marriages and deaths, not merely the indexes, can be consulted in New Register House, Edinburgh. There is, therefore, no need to acquire actual copies of the certificates in order to find out what information the registers contain. Scottish birth and death certificates are also more informative.

Except for a short period in the 1850s, birth certificates record the date and place of the parents' marriage, while death certificates give the names of parents and spouse, if any. There are, indeed, many advantages to the pursuit of genealogy in Scotland.

British subjects who were born, married or died abroad, since 1849, may appear in the Consular Returns at the GRO, and there are also indexes covering registration of the relevant incidents at sea, in the army, etc. Returns for British subjects in India since the late 17th century are to be found in the India Office Library in London. For other parts of what used to be the British Empire, it will probably be necessary to contact the embassy of the country concerned, asking for advice on procedure. In the former dominions of the British Empire, certificates are generally more detailed than the English equivalents. The Canadian Public Archives publish a guide, *Tracing Your Ancestors in Canada*, and there are a large number of similar publications for other countries, including one or two non-English-speaking countries. In some of the less wealthy states, however, adequate systems of central registration do not yet exist.

Right. The unusual circumstances of Henry Crang's death, as reported on his death certificate, suggested a search of the local press might be worthwhile. The report in the *West Somerset Gazette* of 1st September 1883 of the inquest on Henry Crang reveals that he had worked on the railways for 38 years and was deaf.

Below. Certified copy of Henry Crang's death certificate, dated 24th August 1883. Described as a farmer at the time of his marriage, he subsequently joined the railways, a profession that ultimately proved fatal.

SHOCKING FATALITY TO A STATION-MASTER AT BLUE ANCHOR.

Mr. Henry Crang, aged sixty-eight, who had been station-master at Blue Anchor, on the Minehead branch railway, for the past seven years, met with his death in a shocking manner at that station on Friday last. It appears that just before the arrival of the mid-day up train from Minehead, Mr. Crang, as usual, closed the gates at the level crossing below the station, and saw the line clear. He then stopped and looked over the gate on the Blue Anchor side, against which some of the railway men had been at work. He next went towards the line, and as the train approached stooped down over the metals, as though to pick up something, apparently not noticing or hearing the train, owing to his being rather deaf. He was seen by the fireman in this position, but too late to avert the disaster. The unfortunate man was struck by the axle box of one of the front wheels of the engine, and was hurled a distance of five feet into a hole by the side of the railway where the men had been at work. He was picked up and carried into the station, and died shortly afterwards from the injuries he had received. Mr. Crang had been thirty-eight years in the employ of first the Bristol and Exeter and then the Great Western Railway Company, and was afflicted with slight lameness as well as deafness.

An inquest on the body was held on Saturday afternoon, at Mrs. Henson's, the Cleeve Bay hotel, before W. W. Munckton, Esq., coroner for West Somerset. Mr. Manning was appointed foreman of the jury. Mr. Wm. Green, superintendent of police on the Great Western Railway, watched the proceedings on behalf of the company, and Mr. Gibson, traffic manager, of Taunton, was also present. The following evidence was taken:—

Peter Broomfield, fireman on the Great Western Railway, deposed:—The deceased was the station-master at Blue Anchor. On Friday last I left Minehead in the 11.45 a.m up-train, of which I was stoker. The train was about four minutes late. Joseph Jones was the engine driver. Just as we were approaching Blue Anchor station I saw deceased standing clear of the line at the crossing on the station side. When we got within a few yards of the crossing I saw him stoop down and put out his right hand towards the rail, apparently to pick something off the line, and immediately the leading axle box struck him. I turned round to my mate and told him of it, and he at once stopped the train. My mate went back to deceased. We were going slowly at the time, being on the point of stopping. Several men were standing on the same side of the line by the gate, which was shut One of them stood inside the gate, a few yards off from deceased.

Robert Prior said: I am a labourer in the employ of the Great Western Railway Company. I was

---

The Census

The greatest repository of information about individuals and households in the 19th century is the Public Record Office (PRO) in London which, among other records, contains the Census returns.

The purpose of a census is not, of course, to assist later generations of genealogists. It is to compile information about the population and resources of the country which the government wishes to know for administrative purposes. Although it is nowadays thought of as primarily a head count of the population, in former times the word was applied mainly to property, and the purpose was usually one of assessment for taxation. The earliest survey of this kind in England was the *Domesday Book* of 1086, compiled on the orders of William the Conqueror in order to see what he could expect to make out of the nation he had conquered. It is hardly likely that you will need to consult this remarkable compilation; in any case it is totally incomprehensible except to specialists.

But the *Domesday Book* was not the earliest census. According to the Book of Exodus, a count of all males of twenty and over was made by the ancient Israelites to assess their fighting strength. Other ancient societies, including the Persians and the Egyptians, carried out similar surveys but, in the modern sense of the word, the census really dates from Rome. The purpose of the Roman census, supposed to be conducted every five years, was to enumerate the population and assess the prosperity of each family including land, animals, slaves and servants. Under Augustus, the census was extended to the whole empire. It was this, of course, that resulted in Jesus Christ being born in a stable in Bethlehem, the city of David, where Joseph, being of the House of David, had to register.

In modern Europe the first records that amounted to something like a modern census were made in Sweden about the middle of the 17th cen-

tury. In New France (Quebec) a numerical count of individuals and families was in force in the 1660s. In Britain the census came much later. A private bill with government backing was introduced to parliament in 1753 which provided for an annual count of the population and a record of those receiving relief from the parish. It ran into fierce opposition, and was condemned as an attack on 'the last remains of English liberty'. Some people regarded the whole idea with superstitious dread and warned that grave trouble and 'epidemical distemper' would ensue. Others, more rational perhaps, feared it would reveal too much to the nation's enemies. Though passed by the Commons, the bill was thrown out by the House of Lords.

During the next half century, attitudes changed. This was partly a result of the work of Malthus which suggested the advisability of keeping track of population increases relative to the resources available to support it. When the Census bill of 1800 was introduced it passed into law unopposed, though not all critics by any means were silenced. The first Census accordingly took place in the following year, 1801, and a Census has been taken regularly at ten-year intervals ever since, except in 1941 when the British people were preoccupied with other matters.

Since the data required by government varied, the Census returns of different decades give somewhat different kinds of information. Also, one must always bear in mind that the information may not be accurate. The earliest census of any real use to the family historian is the 1841 Census, although a few of the earlier ones are still in existence. As a clear one hundred years has to elapse before the public are allowed to see these records for England and Wales (the rules are different for Scotland), the latest census that can be consulted is the 1881 one.

The Census of 1841 listed every person in every

household by name, approximate age (to the nearest five years), sex and occupation. It also noted whether or not they were born in the same county which, though unfortunately vague, is occasionally a fact worth knowing. It did not give exact addresses nor family relationships; more than one genealogist has slipped up through making the natural assumption that 'George Parker, aged 50' and 'Elizabeth Parker, aged 50' were man and wife when in fact they were brother and sister. However, it is the ages that will give the researcher the most trouble, for although those for children up to the age of 15 had to be accurate, those for adults were to be rounded down to the nearest five years. As so many did not give their correct age anyway (for various reasons), it was possible for someone aged 52 to give the age of 48 which would then be rounded down to 45! Thus, ages quoted in succeeding censuses may not agree.

The 1851 Census is much more informative. It notes addresses by house and street (when possible), and lists everyone staying in the house on the

night of the Census, with their marital status, exact age, occupation and place of birth (exceedingly helpful) if in England or Wales. It identifies the head of the household and the relationship between him and all other individuals under his roof, including servants.

It is important to remember that Census returns, like other records, are subject to human error as well as human dishonesty. The facts were furnished by an ordinary human being, possibly unwell or harassed at the time, subject to forgetfulness, conceivably hostile to the whole notion of a Census, etc. On the whole, people seem to have been remarkably honest and accurate, and the returns were compiled with a great deal of care; however, do not be thrown off balance by inconsistencies in names or dates, and do not take every listed fact as gospel truth. The birth date given for an elderly relative, in particular, is quite likely to be an approximate one.

The Census returns for England and Wales are now mostly on microfilm and are indexed under places. You will probably need some assistance with the machine at first, and it must be said that scanning microfilm is a particularly trying form of research. You will be thankful if the object of your search is soon found. Obviously, you do not want to plough through the records for the whole of a large town if you can avoid it, although as a matter

An extract from the Census returns, 1851. Each member of the household is identified by name and relationship to the head of the family, with age (not always accurate), profession ('scholar', of course, means schoolchild) and place of birth also listed. *PRO ref. no. 170 107/1680.*

of fact this has often been done (you may be lucky: one researcher who had resigned herself to checking every household in Norwich in 1851 actually found what she was looking for within minutes).

If you know the exact address, the problem is an easy one. You may have the correct address as a result of you previous research in the GRO, perhaps from a birth certificate issued near the time of the Census, which gives the address of the parents. Failing that, it might be worth checking a local directory for the district concerned; the best collection of old directories is in the Guildhall Library in London, but local libraries probably have some of the approximate date for their area.

For London and some other large towns, the Census returns are indexed by streets, which makes things easier. Small towns and villages can be scanned surprisingly quickly when you have grown accustomed to the process. Households were larger in the 19th century, and in a village of two or three thousand people you may have to scan only four or five hundred names. There is also always a chance, with these smaller places, of hitting on further useful information by luck – a family of the same name who turn out to be related, for example. Occasionally, when you think you have the right address, you may still fail to locate the family. This is irritating, but a further search often reveals them living not far away, or perhaps staying the night elsewhere in the neighbourhood.

One great advantage of the Census returns is that you can follow developments over a period of time. They also, of course, give a picture of the whole family at the time the Census was taken; it is very likely you will discover previously unknown relatives, or perhaps an elderly aunt whose birth date carries you back some way into the 18th century.

Census returns can be consulted at the Land Registry Building in Portugal Street, London, which is part of the Public Record Office. Although there is no charge for searching, admittance is by pass issued for the day or by reader's ticket. Having found a family in any of the census returns, it is possible to get the appropriate page copied.

Census returns can also be seen in County Record Offices but just for the county in which the Record Office is situated. Local libraries occasionally have copies for their own areas. The Federation of Family History Societies booklet *Census Returns 1841, 1851, 1861 and 1871 on Microfilm – a Directory to Local Holdings* (3rd edition, 1981) will lead you to alternative sites to view the returns, as the office at Portugal Street gets very crowded, especially during the tourist season; unless you have a seat, you cannot start your research. Unfortunately seats cannot be booked in advance. This booklet also lists the whereabouts of any earlier censuses which have survived.

If you cannot find the family living at a particular address in any of the aforementioned censuses but can pin them down to one in 1891 or 1901, it is possible to get minimal information from the Registrar General's Office at St. Catherine's House. If you can prove direct descent and can provide a list of names whom you think might have been living at an exact address in one of these years, the staff will search for you but personal inspection is not allowed. They will only give the age and birthplace of the actual people listed by you so it is advisable to mention as many names as possible.

Scottish Census returns can be inspected at New Register House in Edinburgh, and the Irish returns at the PRO in Dublin. If you have to search for ancestors in Ireland, you will have reason to deplore the disastrous fire which destroyed so many valuable documents in Dublin in 1922. Among the casualties were most of the Census returns from 1861 to 1891 inclusive.

In some of the former colonies and dominions, the Census provided much more detailed information than it did at home. The Census of 1828 in New South Wales, Australia, is a good example. Although the original returns are naturally to be found in Sydney, copies can be inspected at the PRO's new building at Kew. The Canadian Census returns date from 1851, although they are incomplete before 1871. Those who begin their search for British ancestors in the United States will perhaps be disappointed when they cross to this side of the Atlantic, since the U.S. returns are so full of facts, sometimes even noting physical disabilities such as deafness.

Public Record Office

In early Victorian times the national archives of England and Wales were scattered among a variety of places, such as Somerset House and the Tower of London. The Public Record Office was established in Chancery Lane as a central repository in the 1850s, and since then its collection, extensive to begin with, has expanded enormously. The Census returns are kept separately in Portugal Street (not far from Chancery Lane), and a new building was built recently to house certain other records at Ruskin Avenue, Kew (south-west of London). If you intend to visit the PRO for any purpose, the first step, naturally, is to find out which building houses the documents you want to consult. There are equivalent institutions to the London PRO in Edinburgh, for Scotland, and in Belfast and Dublin, for Ireland.

Basically, the PRO contains all government

records over a certain age. The time lapse before a government department hands over its records (other than those which are destroyed) to the PRO varies considerably; one hundred years was at one time the usual period, but in most cases it is now considerably shorter. For instance, a rush of books published on the Second World War in the past few years resulted from the opening of hitherto secret archives relating to that period.

The sheer bulk of material makes the PRO rather an intimidating place; it is no good expecting to accomplish any useful research there, whether in person or through a third party, unless you know exactly what you are looking for. As mentioned earlier, there is a guide to the contents of the PRO published by Her Majesty's Stationery Office. It gives a reasonably detailed description of the main archives, but it is in itself a very substantial publication; at first sight it may prove almost as overwhelming as the thought of those endless piles of paper in the PRO. An even better guide is *Tracing Your Ancestors in The Public Record Office* by Jane Cox and Timothy Padfield (1981) as this has been written specifically for the family historian. Further advice, however, can be obtained from the PRO officials who are not, like a few archivists and librarians, hostile to what must inevitably appear to them as simple-minded inquiries.

For the genealogist, probably the most valuable source in the PRO is the Census returns, as explained in the previous chapter. Other important sources are the Army (War Office) and the Navy (Admiralty) records (see chapter on Trades and Professions). Home Office records contain information about naturalised British subjects as well as about civil servants. There are a number of other sources of considerable general interest, like the records of proceedings in Chancery (disputes over land ownership, etc.), as well as more specialised sources useful in the occasional case.

Anyone who intends to conduct his or her own research at the PRO will need a reader's ticket. If you are trying to trace your ancestors, you are engaged in original research so there should be no difficulty in obtaining a ticket. There are facilities for typing and for tape-recording, but, as in most archival repositories, no pens are allowed; only pencil notes may be taken.

If you are not conducting your own research, you may be able to find out what you want by direct inquiry. As previously explained, the PRO staff cannot undertake lengthy research. However, if your inquiry is a simple one and you are able to provide sufficient data to enable an official acquainted with the documents to go more or less straight to the right place, then the PRO staff will probably undertake to provide the information you require by mail. Similarly, photocopies can be sent by mail, as long as you identify the document you want photocopied and give the correct reference from the official guide.

If a lengthier search is needed, you will have to hire a professional researcher. You will save time and money if you choose someone who is, first, well acquainted with the archives and, second, experienced in genealogical work. A letter to the Keeper of the PRO, stating briefly the research you wish to have done, will elicit some names and addresses of appropriate professional free-lance researchers.

Parish Records

The civil registers of births, marriages and deaths, and the Census returns, together with the private information you started with, ought to have established your descent since the early 19th century. But that is as far as the civil records will take you.

Many of the administrative functions performed today by government were in former times undertaken by the ecclesiastical authorities; it is probably the records of the church, in particular the parish registers, to which you should turn next.

Before you start investigating the English parish registers, you should if possible make sure that your ancestors were members of the Church of England. Not everyone was, of course, even in times when it was, strictly speaking, illegal not to be. If your ancestors were Roman Catholics or belonged to some Non-Conformist sect, you may have to look elsewhere.

From the parish registers you can get the same kind of information as you get from the GRO, except that they go back farther in time. However, they record not births, marriages and deaths but *baptisms*, marriages and *burials*. As a rule, baptism followed birth and burial followed death very quickly, but not always. There are no official records of actual births and deaths before 1837.

The parish registers date back to 1538 in England and Wales, to 1558 in Scotland and to 1634 in Ireland. The idea probably came originally from Spain, as registers of baptisms were made in Castile in 1497. There are in fact one or two English registers of an earlier date than 1538, when the order was made by Thomas Cromwell, on behalf of Henry VIII, which required the weekly register of all baptisms, marriages, and burials. In 1597 parchment books were provided for the registers and it was ordered that transcripts should be made on parchment of all earlier registers on paper. Of the very early registers, it is usually these parchment

copies that have survived. In 1694 a tax on births, marriages and burials was introduced. As a result births as well as baptisms had to be registered, but this lasted only a short time, the objectionable tax being soon rescinded.

Although probably no other country possesses comparable records covering so long a period, the English and Welsh parish registers are naturally incomplete. Even the best-preserved contain gaps in the mid-17th century, during the political turmoil of the Civil War and Commonwealth, when for a time the responsibility of recording baptisms, marriages and burials was removed from the parish priests. Otherwise, the state of the records varies

An extract from the register of baptisms at the church of St Peter and St Paul, Godalming, Surrey for the years 1690–91.

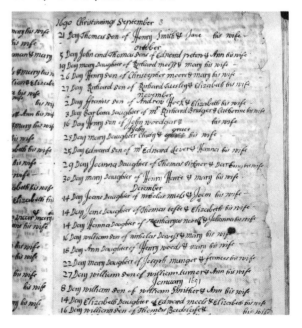

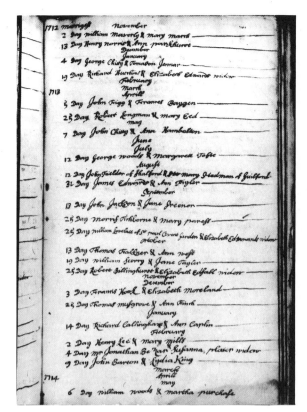

An extract from the register of marriages at the church of St Peter and St Paul, Godalming, Surrey for the years 1688–90.

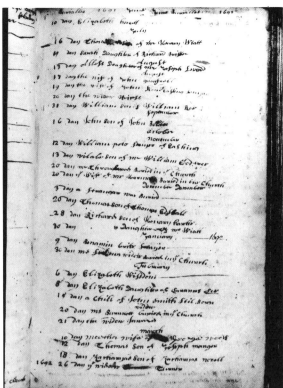

An extract from the register of burials at the church of St Peter and St Paul, Godalming, for the years 1690–92.

from parish to parish. Many do not go back as far as the 16th century, and in some parishes everything has been lost or destroyed through one mishap or another. It is a matter of luck whether the registers in the parish where your ancestors lived are well preserved, but the chances are fairly good that they exist at least since about 1660.

Your first step, however, should be to establish whether the parish in which you are interested still exists. It may have been superseded by a new parish, so the old registers will have to be tracked down. The maps published by the Institute of Heraldic and Genealogical Studies give old parish boundaries and also the dates of the earliest registers in each parish. You should also check that the registers concerned have not been printed. The County Record Office (CRO) will probably be able to tell you; if they have been printed, the CRO should have a copy. There may also be a copy in the library of the Society of Genealogists. The registers themselves may be at the CRO, or they may still be in the care of the parish priest. In a few cases they may be elsewhere; the *National Index of Parish Registers* (edited by D. J. Steel) is the ultimate source for locating them, but this large work is as yet incomplete. In any case you will

probably find it easier to write to the relevant CRO and/or parish priest to inquire.

Although he is no longer so significant a figure as he once was, the parish priest still exists, fortunately for our purposes, and it is sometimes a great advantage to deal with local rectors. Many of them are antiquarians of a sort themselves, and may well prove very helpful in unforeseen ways. If you work by mail, there is a statutory fee for searching the registers. Priests are not well paid and the fees are not large, so private inquirers should show consideration – for example, by enclosing an International Reply Coupon if sending a written inquiry from abroad.

In some parishes you will not be charged any fee if you make the search yourself, though it would be churlish in that case to neglect to make a contribution to church funds. It is certainly advisable to make a personal visit if you can, even if you have already had a search made by someone else, because you may come across other interesting or useful facts in the parish. Besides, to see the church in which your ancestors were baptised, married and buried is hardly less satisfying than discovering their names in the parish registers, and will almost certainly give you some material for your family

A family tomb in the churchyard of St Peter and St Paul, Godalming, which includes four infants who died at less than one year old.

bourhood which you would do well to contact in advance. Local amateur historians are often highly informative and they are also, as a rule, very enthusiastic and eager to assist interested visitors. A large-scale map, preferably one of the earliest Ordnance Survey maps, may also be consulted, along with a tithe map dating from the 1830s (the CRO will probably have a copy).

There may be other clues in the church itself, like a gravestone (they sometimes have most enlightening inscriptions) or a memorial. Gravestones unfortunately are prone to the ravages of time, and old inscriptions are hard to read. Genealogists sometimes arm themselves with a small, softish brush to clean the stone. However, if they are wise they ask first before they start interfering with tombs and gravestones. If your research takes you to Gloucestershire, you are in luck, because the inscriptions in most Gloucester parishes were copied down in the 1780s, with the result that 16th-century inscriptions, which would otherwise have vanished long ago, are permanently preserved. However, family history societies are in the process of recording Monumental Inscriptions (MIs) before the stones deteriorate any further. Contact the appropriate societies for details.

There are many subsidiary church documents, now usually to be found at the CRO, which may provide further facts. The Vestry Minutes contain accounts of parish business, including the appointment of church wardens, accounts for repairs, etc. After the Elizabethan Poor Law came into effect,

history. Apart from the church, the environment may have changed a good deal, but in most places there is something – a view of the hills, an old bridge – which may look much the same to your ancestors as it does to you. Perhaps you will gain new insights, or appreciate hitherto uncomprehended references in old letters, when you visit the home of your ancestors.

If you have been really thorough, you will already have made yourself familiar with the district. Very likely there is a published history of it, which may even mention your ancestors, and there is probably a local history society in the neigh-

Memorial in the church of St Peter and St Paul, Godalming, recording the names of men of the parish – as usual, a ghastly number of them – who died in the First World War. They are helpful if you cannot find any record of a dead relative who you know lived in the parish.

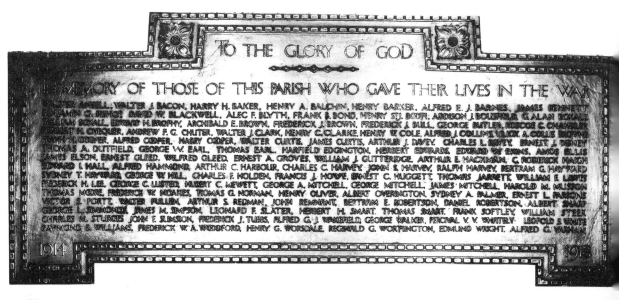

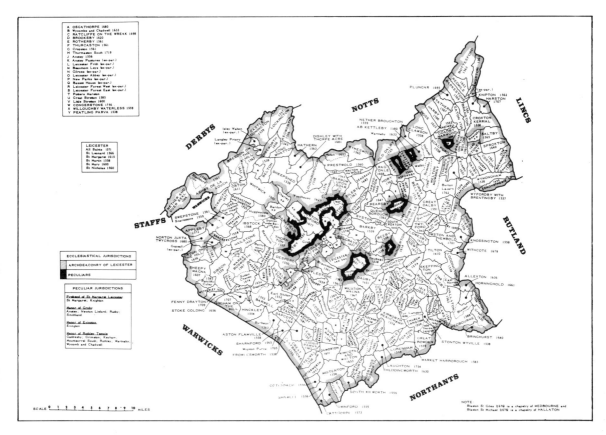

Above. Parish map of the county of Leicestershire, published by the Institute of Heraldic and Genealogical Studies in Canterbury. These maps are invaluable for establishing the relevant ecclesiastical authority. Note the large numbers of 'Peculiars' (an unusual type of religious authority).

Below. Extract from the Vestry Minutes in the parish of Richmond, Surrey. An increasing number of these parish records have been printed, though in most cases it is still necessary to consult the original document. From *The Richmond Vestry Minutes: Extracts from the Notes of its History and Operations 1614–1890*.

the Overseers of the Poor in each parish kept a record of their accounts. Indeed, if one of your ancestors had the misfortune to be a pauper, the chance of finding traces of him may be better than if he were more prosperous. It was the task of each parish to deal with its own poor, and the records of Settlement and Removal are concerned with attempts to return such people to the appropriate parish.

People often tend to assume that if they can locate their ancestors around two hundred years ago living in an English village, then they have only to look through the parish records to trace the family back another couple of centuries. This can happen, but it is actually rather unusual. Although people moved about less then they have done in more recent generations, they did not all stay in the same spot indefinitely. If you find your family in the same place for more than two consecutive generations, you should consider yourself lucky. When they did move, however, they often moved only a short distance, and a search among the

OFFICERS AND STAFF.

The following is a list of the paid Officers and Employés of the Vestry at 1st November, 1890, and their respective remunerations:—

	Salary.	
	£ s. d.	£ s. d.
Mr. F. B. Senior.*		
As Clerk to Urban Sanitary Authority	450 0 0	
As Vestry Clerk	50 0 0	
As Clerk to School Attendance Committee	50 0 0	
As Clerk to Baths Committee	20 0 0	
As Clerk to Fire Brigade Committee	10 10 0	
As Clerk to Burial Board (⅔rds of £25)	16 13 4	
		597 3 4

* £105 additional was paid in 1890 for special services in connection with Lower George Street Improvements.

	£ s. d.
Mr. W. Brooke.	
Town Surveyor	500 0 0
Assistants and Clerks	250 0 0
Mr. J. E. Broderick.	
Road Foreman (with residence) ...	136 10 0
Mr. W. Penn-Lewis.†	
Accountant	250 0 0
Additional, re Burial Board ...	8 6 8
Accountant's Clerk	39 0 0

† £25 extra was paid at Easter, 1890, for special services during the previous year.

neighbouring parishes may reveal their presence.

If the parish registers are missing or incomplete, do not despair. From the late 16th century annual returns of baptisms, marriages and burials had to be made to the diocesan authorities (a diocese is the province of a bishop). They are known as Bishop's Transcripts, and they are usually to be found nowadays at the CRO (if not, the CRO will be able to tell you where they are). Sometimes the Bishop's Transcripts have survived when the parish registers are missing, though on the whole these records reveal more gaps than the registers. They may contain entries which for some reason were not made in the parish register, or additional information not included in the original entry, so it is often worth checking them anyway. Remember, though, that in the days before photocopying, overworked or inefficient clerks often made copying errors.

If you are unable to find a record of a marriage in the parish register even though you are reasonably certain that it took place, you may be able to trace it through the banns – public proclamation of a forthcoming marriage, compulsory since 1754 and often found earlier. The Banns Books will probably be in the same place as the registers.

Banns have to be proclaimed in church on three different Sundays. If a couple wished to get married quickly, they could dispense with this process by obtaining a marriage licence. A licence was also needed at one period if the marriage took place during Lent. This procedure became more fashionable among those who could afford the extra expense it involved, whether they were in a hurry or not, and regardless of the time of year. As it is the universal custom of people to ape their supposed betters, and as the expense of a marriage licence was not very great, most people with middle-class pretentions tended to get married by licence, even a lawyer's clerk like Mr Wemmick in *Great Expectations*.

Marriage licences were obtained from the bishop if bride and bridegroom came from the same diocese. If they came from different dioceses in the same province, a Vicar-general licence was required – from the Vicar-general of the archbishop of Canterbury or York. If the two dioceses were in different provinces (Canterbury and York), then a Faculty Office licence was required – from the master of faculties of the archbishop of Canterbury. Certain other ecclesiastical officials also had the right to issue marriage licences.

A marriage licence is a considerable advantage in genealogical research. For one thing, such marriages are on the whole easier to trace. To obtain a licence, it was necessary to provide a statement known as an 'allegation' from the bride and bridegroom as well as assurances called bonds from the bondsmen, usually relatives or friends. These do-cuments normally contain more information than is to be found on marriage certificates. They were originally deposited in the Diocesan Record Office, which today means (usually) the CRO. Some marriage licences have been published by county record societies and similar bodies; the CRO will be able to tell you if this is so in the area in which you are interested.

The Church of the Latter-Day Saints, or Mormon Church, has a special interest in genealogy. The Mormons have a vast amount of the parish registers of England and Wales, as well as other countries, on microfilm in their library in Salt Lake City. There are copies in other Mormon libraries and also in the Society of Genealogists' Library in London, while local record offices have microfiches for their own districts. The Mormons' interest is in baptising their ancestors by proxy according to the rites of their Church, and therefore they do *not* include burial registers, though there are some marriages. Their work has made the genealogist's task much easier, because whereas it was formerly necessary to search painfully through the registers parish by parish, the computer index to the Mormon parish register collection can now reveal the wanted entry in a matter of seconds. However, not all the parish or Non-Conformist registers are included and where they are, there is not neccessarily a coverage for the whole period of the register. Therefore, you may be lucky in finding the appropriate entry (there are 25 million entries in the British index), but it must be remembered that this index is a *finding aid only* and the original registers should be checked. And so, when you are moving on from civil registers and census returns to parish registers, it would probably be a good idea to consult the computer index (known as the International Genealogical Index).

However, on the whole marriage registers are the most reliable of the parish records; baptismal registers are slightly less useful if only because not everyone was baptised (not everyone was married either, but the proportion is smaller). Burial registers are not particularly informative, but they can assist, for example, in distinguishing between two children of the same name in one family (not uncommon when one died young) and also in guiding your search for a will, which may well be the next step in your research.

Welsh parish registers and Bishop's Transcripts are in the National Library of Wales, Aberystwyth, whilst in Scotland parish registers can be consulted in New Register House, Edinburgh. In Ireland, apart from those still held by the ecclesiastical authorities, a great number were destroyed by the fire of 1922. Some Anglican churches abroad may hold registers, and you can inquire for possible transcripts of these at the Guildhall Library.

Dissenters, i.e. non-members of the Church of England, will often be found in the parish registers. A law of 1753 enforced their marriage in the parish church (though Jews and Quakers were later excepted) and births as well as marriages are sometimes found at an earlier date: the purpose was to ensure legal confirmation of these events, important for future inheritance of property. Even after the 1753 Act, however, many Dissenters' marriages were not recorded except by their own sects.

Most of these records are now in the PRO, including a large number of secret marriages which took place from the late 17th to the mid-18th centuries. They vary a good deal in usefulness, since many of the records have been destroyed. The best

Computer print-out from the International Genealogical Index compiled by the Mormons which often provides a vital short-cut when searching parish records, especially for baptisms. Nowadays, the next step after civil registrations and census returns is to consult the IGI, but only as an index to registers; the relevant parish records must then be sought.

are those of the Society of Friends, or Quakers, who maintained accurate records of births, marriages and deaths from the mid-17th century. Digests of these registers, indexed by county, can be inspected in the Society of Friends' library, as well as the PRO. Other Protestant Non-Conformist records of baptisms and burials do not, as a rule, go back so far. Although the PRO is the place to apply first, some may be found in the local CRO and some remain in the possession of the chapels. It is in any case worthwhile contacting these chapels or, if they no longer exist, the headquarters of the group concerned, because there may be earlier records which were not collected at the time civil registers came into effect. Dr Williams Library in London has some registers of Dissenters' births from 1752 to 1837, mostly from congregations in London; the register of burials at Bunhill Fields, the great Non-Conformist cemetery, is available in print from the Guildhall Library. Other institutions likely to help are the Methodists' Research Centre and the Congregational Historical Society.

Jewish records of births, marriages and deaths

COUNTRY: ENGLAND	COUNTY: STAFFORD			AS OF OCT 1976					PAGE 244		
NAME	SEX:M MALE/F FEMALE/H HUSBAND/W WIFE FATHER/MOTHER OR SPOUSE	T Y P E	EVENT DATE	TOWN, PARISH	B	E	S	SOURCE BATCH	SERIAL SHEET
ALLEN, JOHN									
ALLEN, JOHN	MARY FOXALL	M M	27NOV1703	WOLVERHAMPTON			13JUL1973PV	7254825	11
ALLEN, JOHN	MARY GARROTT	M M	23JUL1704	HARBORNE			18AUG1972O6	7205519	99
ALLEN, JOHN	WILLIAM ALLEN?	M C	18MAR1705	BURSLEM	D8NOV1932	13DEC1934SL	28JAN1969L6	P010041	2415
ALLEN, JOHN	THOS./ANNAE	M C	24MAR1705	STOKE UPON TRENT	27JAN1966BM	29MAR1966SL	09MAR1972SL	P009961	4813
ALLEN, JOHN	HAMPTON HOLLINSHEAD	M M	23MAY1705	ASHLEY		·	CLEARED	M009961	0958
ALLEN, JOHN	MARY HICKMANS	M M	30APR1710	TETTENHALL			18MAY1961IF	A459127	1399
ALLEN, JOHN	BENJ./ANNAE	M C	07JUL1711	STOKE UPON TRENT	12DEC1953	08FEB1956AZ	13MAR1972SL	P009961	5433
ALLEN, JOHN	WILLIAM ALLEN	M C	19DEC1719	PENKRIDGE	22DEC1965LA	25MAR1966LA	14APR1969L6	P010521	4902
ALLIN, JOHN	SARAH COPE	M M	08JUN1721	KINGSLEY			13JUN1972SL	7116405	54
ALLEN, JOHN	SAMUEL ALLEN/CATHERINE	M C	19MAY1723	WOLSTANTON	D5MAR1938	17MAR1938AZ	05DEC1968AZ	P010031	4388
ALLEN, JOHN	MARY DRENN	M M	05NOV1723	TETTENHALL			18MAY1961IF	A459127	1398
ALLEN, JOHN	ALICE RATCLIFFE	M M	05JUN1728	ASHLEY			CLEARED	M060891	3222
ALLEN, JOHN	ELIZABETH COPE	M C	07OCT1728	DILHORNE			13JUN1972SL	7116405	55
ALLEN, JOHN	ELIZABETH COPE	M C	07OCT1728	DILHORNE			22JUL1969L6	A537764	2064
ALLEN, JOHN	JOHN ALLEN/MARY	M C	23OCT1729	TETTENHALL	15OCT1960	15NOV1960AZ	04JAN1968SL	P010671	3679
ALLEN, JOHN	JANE HANSON	M M	18DEC1732	TATENHILL			07FEB1973S6	7223622	80
ALLEN, JOHN	MARY THORNTON	M M	30DEC1732	ASHLEY			CLEARED	M060891	3710
ALLEN, JOHN	ELIZABETH FRADLEY	M M	26MAY1735	ASHLEY			CLEARED	M060891	3803
ALLEN, JOHN	MATTHEW/MARY	M C	17OCT1737	BILSTON	02APR1960	26APR1960SL	P010561	2667
ALLEN, JOHN	WILLIAM ALLEN/JANE	M C	04MAR1739	WOLSTANTON	18AUG1965SL	10NOV1965SL	11DEC1968AZ	P010031	5042
ALLEYNE, JOHN	GEORGE ALLEYNE/EMMA	M C	12JUN1740	ABBOTS BROMLEY	CLEARED	CLEARED	CLEARED	C035162	2623
ALLEN, JOHN	THOS. ALLEN/ELIZ.	M C	25APR1741	STOKE UPON TRENT	28JAN1966SL	05APR1966SL	18JUL1968L6	P009961	8749
ALLEN, JOHN	RALPH ALLEN/ELLEN	M C	11MAR1743	BURSLEM	14DEC1937	05JAN1938SL	29JAN1969L6	P010041	4130
ALLEN, JOHN	JOHN/ANNE	M C	28DEC1753	BILSTON	02APR1960	27APR1960SL	27AUG1969NZ	P010561	3438
ALLEN, JOHN	SAML. ALLEN/ANN	M C	07JUL1754	TATENHILL,SAINT MICHAEL	D6NOV1965MT	07JAN1966MT	11JUL1968AZ	P009841	2400
ALLEN, JOHN	JANE TURNER	M M	05NOV1754	WEDNESBURY			10DEC1971IF	7100617	80
ALLEN, JOHN	ELIZABETH INGLEY	M M	07MAY1755	WALSALL			20JAN1955IF	A459815	0311
ALLEN, JOHN	ELIZABETH DUDLEY	M M	28JUL1757	UTTOXETER			CLEARED	7424612	49
ALLEN, JOHN	MARY ALLCOCK	M M	27NOV1758	DILHORNE			CLEARED	7424612	54
ALLEN, JOHN	MARY JONES	M M	30JUL1759	HAUGHTON			06DEC1972L6	7134015	64
ALLEN, JOHN	MARY JONES	M M	30JUL1759	HAUGHTON			26JUN1963SL	A457863	0400
ALLEN, JOHN	THOMAS ALLEN/MARY	M C	04MAR1760	UTTOXETER	CLEARED	CLEARED	CLEARED	7424113	18
ALLEN, JOHN	JOHN ALLEN/ELIZABETH	M C	03APR1760	UTTOXETER	CLEARED	CLEARED	CLEARED	7424113	19
ALLEN, JOHN	ANN COX	M M	13JUL1763	SEDGLEY			26JUN1973SL	7226504	52
ALLEN, JOHN	WILLIAM/SARAH	M C	20JAN1765	SEDGLEY	21MAR1973L6	17MAY1973L6	31MAR1973L6	7227971	53
ALLEN, JOHN	JOHN ALLEN/ANN	M C	05NOV1765	STAFFORD,SAINT CHAD	29NOV1965SL	14JAN1966SL	24SEP1968NZ	P010231	0877
ALLIN, JOHN	JOHN ALLEN/ANN	M C	08FEB1767	DILHORNE	INFANT	INFANT	CLEARED	7424111	27
ALLIN, JOHN	WM. ALLIN/	M C	02JUL1769	NEWCASTLE UNDER LYME	15OCT1960	16NOV1960AZ	27MAR1972SL	P010291	0823
ALLIN, JOHN	ELES WILLIAM/ELEANOR	M C	03DEC1769	WEST BROMWICH	22APR1972LA	05OCT1972LA	23MAR1973LA	7125015	12
ALLIN, JOHN	JOSEPH ALLIN/	M C	14MAR1773	NEWCASTLE UNDER LYME	INFANT	INFANT	06JAN1969SL	P010291	1364
ALLEN, JOHN	JAMES ALLEN/HANNAH	M C	20MAR1774	ELLASTONE	27NOV1954	22FEB1955SL	20DEC1968AZ	P010101	4168
ALLEN, JOHN	THOMAS ALLEN/ELIZABETH	M C	23MAY1779	BASWICH	02APR1960	27APR1960SL	17OCT1968L6	P011031	1987
ALLEN, JOHN	CATHERINE BIDDLE	M M	23MAY1779	WALSALL			14OCT1972SO6	7501402	78
ALLEN, JOHN	ANN BAGNALL	M M	07OCT1787	ASHLEY			CLEARED	M009961	4037
ALLIN, JOHN	JOHN ALLEN/ANN	M C	25FEB1787	BURSLEM	26SEP1960	02NOV1960SL	29JAN1969L6	P010041	9168
ALLEN, JOHN	/MARY ALLIN/	M C	10APR1787	NEWCASTLE UNDER LYME	D2MAR1967SL	22MAR1967SL	27MAR1972SL	P010291	3539
ALLEN, JOHN	MARTHA HAMMERSLY	M M	01OCT1787	STOKE UPON TRENT			11MAY1961IF	A459127	0992
ALLEN, JOHN	MARTHA WHEELDON	M M	09FEB1789	ALSTONFIELD			04JUN1959AZ	A456369	0416
ALLEN, JOHN	JOHN ALLEN/ANN	M C	01FEB1790	UTTOXETER	INFANT	INFANT	CLEARED	C047951	2028
ALLEN, JOHN	WILLIAM ALLEN/ANN	M C	03AUG1791	UTTOXETER	INFANT	INFANT	CLEARED	C047951	2341
ALLEN, JOHN	JOHN ALLEN/MARTHA	M C	07AUG1791	STOKE UPON TRENT	15OCT1960	15NOV1960AZ	23JUL1968L6	P009961	4567
ALLEN, JOHN	OLIVE PICKHORN	M M	23APR1792	ASHLEY			CLEARED	M009961	5040
ALLEN, JOHN	WILLIAM ALLEN/ANN	M C	15SEP1792	UTTOXETER	CLEARED	CLEARED	CLEARED	C047951	2345
ALLEN, JOHN	SARAH COLLINS	M M	20MAY1794	SEDGLEY			29MAY1973PV	7230424	62
ALLEN, JOHN	JAS ALLEN/SARAH	M C	11MAY1794	CHEDDLETON	16APR1975WA	15JUL1975WA	CLEARED	7424112	77
ALLEN, JOHN	WILLIAM ALLEN/MARY	M C	01MAR1795	WOLVERHAMPTON,SAINT PETER AND SAINT PAUL-RC	29JUL1969L6	10NOV1969L6	18NOV1969L6	P015371	0095
ALLEN, JOHN	JOHN ALLEN/ANN	M C	26MAR1797	UTTOXETER	CLEARED	CLEARED	CLEARED	C047951	3165
ALLEN, JOHN	WILLIAM ALLEN/ELIZABETH	M C	08NOV1797	STAFFORD,SAINT MARY	CLEARED	CLEARED	CLEARED	C010221	1031

B=BIRTH, C=CHRISTENING, M=MARRIAGE, N=CENSUS, W=WILL ALL OTHERS =MISCELLANEOUS contain more information than Christian ones. The majority of Jewish immigrants to England arrived in comparatively recent times, and their ancestry must be traced, if possible, in their countries of origin. However, there are some English Jews whose ancestors arrived as long ago as the mid-17th century, when Jews were re-admitted for the first time since the 13th century. The Jewish Historical Society or the Jewish Museum, both in London, will try to put you on the right course to locate the records, which are not to be found in the PRO.

Roman Catholic registers in the 16th and 17th centuries had to be kept in secret, and most of them have inevitably disappeared. Surviving registers were not handed over when civil registration began at the beginning of Queen Victoria's reign, and therefore they are mostly to be found still in the hands of the individual churches. A few have been published by the Catholic Record Society.

County Record Offices

In recent years the City, Borough or County Record Office (CRO) has become the main archival repository outside the PRO in London, and a great deal of research at local level is done there. CROs are a comparative innovation; the earliest, Bedford, was founded in 1914 and it was not until after the Second World War that they became common. Some CROs are more efficient or better equipped than others, and not everyone approves of the centralization of records in these, or any other offices. On the other hand, it is obviously convenient to have all related records in one place where a high standard of conservation and a highly trained, strongly motivated staff are available. On the other hand, an untimely accident such as a fire or a bomb is all the more disastrous.

Some CROs undertake a tremendous amount of work, dealing with as many as a thousand inquiries, by mail, telephone or personal visit, every month, as well as issuing a large number of their own publications. Some of them have produced guides or reports on their holdings, and if you anticipate any research, by mail or in person, at a particular CRO, it will be useful to examine the relevant guide, if one exists, before you do so.

Some of these guides are very detailed. For example, *The Genealogist's Guide to the West Sussex Record Office* by Peter M. Wilkinson (West Sussex County Council, 1979) includes a comprehensive list of what is available from parish registers, whether in the form of originals, Bishop's Transcripts, microfilm copies or modern transcripts. There are registers from about 85 per cent of the parishes in West Sussex, most of them starting before 1600. The list is arranged alphabetically by parish and indicates dates and types (whether original registers, transcripts, etc.), and whether indexed or not. The existence of recorded memorial inscriptions (gravestones, etc.) is also noted, and a separate list gives the parishes for which such inscriptions are recorded, the name of the person who transcribed them and where they are to be found. There is a separate list of Non-Conformist and Roman Catholic registers, and notes of a variety of other records, such as cemetery registers, school admission registers, indexes of wills and other probate records. Also included are microfilm census returns for West Sussex, as well as lists of other sources, including printed books, for genealogical research. There is even a parish map of the county. In short, anyone intending to initiate genealogical research in the West Sussex CRO can find out in advance exactly what records the office holds and can be as certain as it is possible to be whether he will find what he is looking for.

Not all CROs publish such useful guides. If none is available it is best to make preliminary inquiries of the County Archivist, who will also be able to advise, if necessary, on the extent to which his or her staff can undertake research on your behalf.

Some records which you might in a general way expect to find at the CRO are not in fact there. They may be in some rather obscure archive elsewhere, but in that case the CRO will almost certainly be able to tell you exactly where they are. Failing that, try the National Register of Archives in London, which attempts to keep lists of all archives throughout the country which may have some national significance, extending to diaries of individuals as well as records of public bodies of various kinds.

A good deal of confusion has been caused by the reorganization of local government in 1974, which altered many old county boundaries. The CROs are of course concerned with historical records, and as a rule their holdings represent the pre-1974 boundaries, except for material published since that date.

The Diocesan Record Offices are now in most cases amalgamated with the CRO. Besides the copies of parish registers known as Bishop's Transcripts, they contain records of church courts and the local clergy.

Unfortunately many CROs are having to cut down their services to the public at present, brought about by harsh financial cuts. This has resulted in hours (in some cases days) of opening having to be curtailed. Therefore it is important to write ahead of time to confirm hours of opening and to book a seat to avoid disappointment on arrival.

Research

Some people have a natural gift for research. Whether you do or do not possess the ingrained traits of a good researcher, there are certain desirable qualities which you should try to cultivate.

The first of these is precision. It is unnecessary to explain why accuracy is essential; obviously, you are in serious trouble if you write a name down incorrectly. However, what is required is the cultivation of an attitude of mind in which pedantic accuracy comes naturally. Most people, reading a report in a newspaper for example, are familiar with the sensation, 'I have read that somewhere before'. In research, you must know, or be able to find out, exactly where you read it. It is no good recollecting, 'It was that day I spent in the London Library', or 'It was in that fat book with the blue cover'. You should know name, author and perhaps section of the book, if not the actual page number.

With precision, you should nourish the natural human instinct for order. Nothing is more infuriating than a long search for a set of notes which have been misplaced, unless it is discovering an important note with no record of where it came from or what it refers to. You should establish a regular system of working and stick to it. If the system ultimately proves unsatisfactory for some reason, of course you will have to work out a new one, but do not simply adapt your method of working as you go along. A temporary convenience may turn out in the long run to be a permanent hazard.

The virtues of precision, order and control must be exercised when you are consulting old indexes, calendars of documents and reference books. After a couple of hours spent examining old registers or trade directories, when tiredness and boredom may begin to affect you, it is all too easy to make a mistake by missing out a line, or by linking two facts incorrectly as a result of overlooking a badly printed punctuation mark.

Archives and reference libraries can themselves be bewildering places until you grow familiar with their organization. Despite incidental oddities and idiosyncrasies, they generally work according to a logical system, and if the librarian can understand it, so can you! Although help is usually at hand if you do get lost, you do not want to keep running to the librarian every few minutes.

To be precise, you must also endeavour to be unbiased, or at least aware of your own bias. Most people, although they know from their daily papers how the facts of a situation can be coloured by the manner of reporting, are not sufficiently aware of the danger when consulting old books and documents. No one sets out on any research assignment without some preconceived ideas, and, as history books show, it is usually possible to find facts to fit a hypothesis, however outrageous. Two historians, using identical source material, may come to completely different conclusions about the nature of a particular incident or individual. And so, if you set out with too firm a notion of what you are going to find, you will automatically tend to discount, consciously or not, facts which contradict that notion. If you are convinced that a certain famous man was your ancestor, your eye will alight eagerly on any item which tends to corroborate your belief, and pass glassily over some equally significant fact which does not.

In letters, diaries or printed books, there are two sets of prejudices to be borne in mind – your own and the writer's. These prejudices may be personal or they may simply reflect current conventions. The statement that a certain man was of grossly immoral character may mean that he was a convicted rapist or it may mean that now and then he took a little too much to drink; it depends on the views of the author of the statement. Private documents, such as letters and diaries, naturally tend to be more subjective than statements written for

Plate 16.

Plate 8.

A list of Christian names and names of counties showing some of the ways such names were abbreviated in old documents. From A. Wright's *Court Hand Restored*, 1818.

publication. Allowances must be made for contemporary custom and changing ideas. The generally accepted beliefs of any previous age contain many ingredients that to us are unpleasant or downright wrong, but they must be accepted as normal within their historical context. The diary of a colonial official in the 19th century is likely to betray an assumption that the local inhabitants are socially or intellectually inferior to their alien rulers, but to condemn the writer as a racist is merely to condemn the generally accepted beliefs of his time.

Although it is important to maintain a logical and neutral attitude to the material, this should not mean that all imagination is suppressed. The mind should be open, so that the significance of possible clues is not missed, and possibly rewarding inferences can be drawn from the bare facts.

For example, a 19th-century diary contained a number of references to a friend of the diarest described only by his initials, J.S., whom it was important to identify. The facts that could be learned about him, except that he was a friend and neighbour of the diarist, were very sparse. However, two or three incidents reported in the diary, such as the gift from J.S. of a box of tea, offered a strong hint as to his trade. A contemporary trade directory of the town concerned contained two grocers with the initials J.S. One of these was ruled out when he was found to have died at an earlier date than the last reference to J.S. in the diary. The other, Joseph Simpson, seemed to be the man, and further research revealed that a son of the diarist had married a daughter of this Joseph Simpson at a later date not covered by the diary. The marriage certificate was the last piece of evidence, proving conclusively the identity of J.S. A crucial clue in this little detective puzzle was the gift of tea, which a less imaginative researcher might have failed to follow up.

The golden rule when consulting old records is to take nothing on trust. Names, dates and other facts may have been recorded incorrectly through clerical error, lack of information or, occasionally, deliberate intent to deceive.

If you are not accustomed to dealing with them, you may find that parish registers and similar documents are rather hard to read. Old handwriting, though in general more carefully composed than ours, can appear indecipherable at first glance. You will probably not have the time or inclination to make a serious study of palaeography (ancient writing and scripts), but if you are going to do any research among old records yourself, you must have at least some knowledge of different styles of handwriting, which, incidentally, is sometimes useful in dating a particular document. The letters were formed in different ways at different periods, and it is not too hard a task to make yourself familiar with these conventions. Most people are aware of the old custom, still to be found one hundred years ago, of writing an *s* rather like an *f*, of writing *i* and *j* interchangeably, or of writing *th* as *y* ('Ye Old Teashoppe' was *not* pronounced as spelled!). There are a number of similar, common conventions which are worth knowing. Your local library will probably have books on handwriting, of which there are several quite easily available. Another useful aid in this connection is *How to Read Local Archives 1550–1700*, F. G. Emmison (1978).

Another problem which crops up occasionally is the use of shorthand. For instance, it can be seen in minutes of inquests and legal proceedings generally, and sometimes in personal diaries and other documents. Shorthand first came into relatively common use in the 17th century – Samuel Pepys was a notable practitioner – and it sometimes took idiosyncratic forms which demand considerable time and effort to decipher.

In the rather unlikely event of your search carrying you back into the Middle Ages, you will find the documents written in Latin; in fact, this is usually the case with manorial records as late as the first third of the 18th century. They are sometimes easier to translate than you might suppose, as the clerks often knew little more classical Latin than you (probably!) do; when stuck for a word they adopted an English one. There are, again, books to help you, such as *Record Interpreter* by C. T. Martin (1949), but if you have to deal with any very lengthy document in Latin, you should, naturally, seek more expert advice.

When noting dates before the year 1752, it is important to remember that in England the (Old Style) Julian calendar was still in use, whereas most of the Continent had adopted the (New Style) Gregorian calender in 1582, as had Scotland in 1660. Moreover, to add to the confusion, the Old Style calender started on the 25th March instead of the 1st January. Some people realised that England was out of step and this is echoed in some registers which record two dates, e.g. 23rd August 1718/19 (i.e. 1718 Old Style and 1719 New Style).

By 1751, the Old Style calender was incorrect by 11 days, so an act of parliament, dated that year, decreed that this should be changed: not only the following 1st January should become the first day of 1752, but that 2nd September should be followed the next day by 14th September. The effect was as follows: 1750 started on 25th March 1750 and ended on 24th March 1751; 1751 started 25th March 1751 and ended 31st December 1751; 1752 started 1st January 1752 and ended 31st December 1752, with 11 days in September missing. When noting down dates earlier than 1752 it is advisable to make a habit of adding (OS) or (NS) as appropriate.

Wills

If you can locate the will of some ancestor, you may find it contains a good deal of unexpected information which will be welcome in providing a fuller picture of his life than any other formal document is likely to do. In your research so far, you will for the most part have been recovering facts of a broadly predictable kind. Although you may also have learned or surmised some facts that could not have been guessed, you will usually have known more or less exactly where to look for the documents concerned. Wills are rather different. Locating them can be complicated, and until you have located them you will have little idea of how much, or how little, help they will provide.

A will tells you when a person died and what his and occasionally her – married women owned nothing before the Married Women's Property Act of 1882 – material circumstances were. As a rule it will give you some idea of what sort of life he led, where he lived, and perhaps what his occupation was. Wills are sometimes accompanied by other documents, such as an inventory of the possessions of the deceased made by the executors after his death, which can be most valuable. Often, when there was no will, you may find a bond of administration, sometimes called an 'admon', which is a document authorising disposal of the property by the next-of-kin. Alternatively you might find a deposition – a statement made by a dying person before witnesses in lieu of a proper will.

A will can bring you suddenly closer to your ancestors than any of the relatively impersonal documents described so far. They may be humorous, pathetic or downright malignant. You may come across odd bequests, hard to understand (why did Shakespeare leave Anne Hathaway his second-best bed?), or merely evidence of eccentricity. First, however, you must find the will.

For wills proved since 1858 there is no problem.

Beginning in that year, wills in England and Wales were proved in the Principal Probate Registry at Somerset House or at a District Probate Registry. In either case, they are indexed at the Principal Probate Registry and, as long as you remember that wills and admons are in separate volumes (until 1870), it is a fairly simple matter to locate them even if you do not know the exact date of death. In fact, providing you are sure there *was* a will, it is quicker to locate a death date via a will than by the indexes to death certificates in the GRO, as you have to consult only one volume per year instead of one per quarter. Having located the will, your best course is to secure a photocopy, which Probate Registries will provide for a modest fee.

Before 1858, matters are unfortunately much more complicated. Before you set out on your search you would be wise to study the problem of locating wills in rather more detail than can be provided here. Reliable guides are *Wills and Their Whereabouts* by A. J. Camp (1974) and *Wills and Where to Find Them* by J. S. W. Gibson (1974). If you are restricted by time or distance, or if your nerve fails you when you contemplate the nature of the task ahead, and – not the least important qualification – if you are prepared to spend a certain amount of money on your hunt, you may decide to hire a professional genealogist to undertake the search. Someone who is familiar with this complex field of research will be able to complete the task much more quickly than an amateur.

Before the civil probate registries were created, the proving of wills was church business, and wills must be sought through the church courts. At first acquaintance these courts – nearly 400 of them – may appear rather bewildering. However, it does not take long to become familiar with the system, and in the majority of cases the will is now to be found in some civil repository such as the CRO.

If a man's property lay entirely within one archdeaconry, his will was, in the normal course of events, proved in the relevant archdeacon's court. If his property was in more than one archdeaconry but all in the same diocese, his will was proved in the bishop's court. If his property was in more than one diocese, his will was proved in one of the two archbishops' courts, the Prerogative Court of Canterbury (PCC) or the Prerogative Court of York (PCY). If he had property in both provinces (Canterbury and York), then his will was proved in the senior court of Canterbury, which also proved wills of English property owners who died abroad and *all* wills for a period during the Commonwealth.

This is all quite logical and straightforward. The main difficulty, of course, lies in the fact that you may well not know in which category your ancestor's property fell, and therefore cannot safely rule out any of the alternatives. Moreover, even if the will concerned fell into the first category and could have been proved in the archdeacon's court, this did not necessarily happen. There was a tendency,

up to about 1800, for reasonably well-off people to have wills proved in a higher court, particularly the PCC. Exactly why they adopted this practice, which involved them in some extra expense, is a matter of argument; no doubt the higher court carried greater authority in the event of later disputes and, as it was normally farther away, greater privacy. The provisions of wills tend to encourage the nastier sort of gossip, and even the most innocuous bequests can invite resentment. Wills are not private documents, and if proved locally could be the more easily inspected by ill-disposed persons.

Another problem in ascertaining where a will was proved arises from the fact that not every parish or district was subject to the authority of the archdeaconry or diocese in which it was situated.

An extract from the will of John Bull, dated 1772 and proved in the Prerogative Court of Canterbury on the 21st October 1776. *Prob 11/1024.*

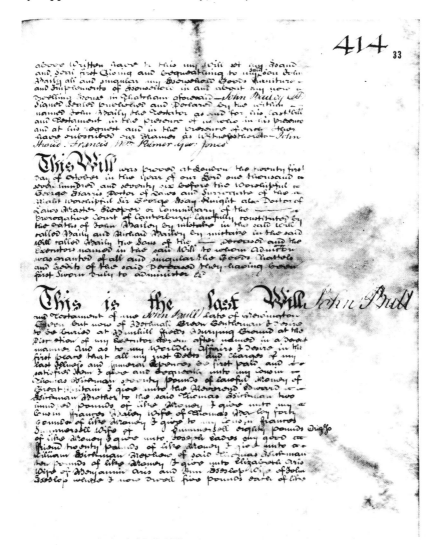

These districts, called 'peculiars', mostly originated in grants made to individuals for services to the Crown a very long time ago, and they are scattered quite thickly across the ecclesiastical maps (they can be identified on the maps published by the Institute of Heraldic and Genealogical Studies). The will of a person owning property in a peculiar could not, as a rule, be proved in the local archdeacon's court and it is not always immediately obvious in what court it was proved – in many cases the PCC but sometimes in a quite unexpected court.

Another factor that has to be borne in mind is that wills were not always proved in the court, whether archdeacon's or bishop's, where the death occurred. If the executors lived in another part of the country, they might find it more convenient to have the will proved in their own area.

Sometimes a long period elapsed before a will was proved, and you should not give up the search if you cannot find a record of your ancestor's will in the year he died. It may have been proved several years later.

Wills of people on the female side of the family, with a different surname, are worth tracing as they are likely to mention members of the family with which you are specifically concerned. The wills of neighbours may also be interesting. All this takes a great deal of time, however, and you will have to decide how widely you are going to cast your net on the basis of the time you have available.

Wills can be extremely long documents, including in them a lot of repetitive legal jargon. When ordering a photocopy you may well decide that only certain parts are necessary, though of course this is almost impossible to decide if you have not already seen the will. In any case, you should scrutinise the whole document with care, because it may reveal all kinds of unexpected information besides such obvious facts as name, address and occupation of the person concerned, his property and possessions, debts and investments and (probably) his relatives, servants, tenants, etc. If you can discover a series of wills, you will have a better picture of your ancestors' way of life than any other standard source is likely to provide.

The search for a will is one of the most exciting tasks in your whole project. It may turn out to be the most important, though it can also be the most frustrating, as the search may be long and the result negative.

Where should you begin? Probably it is best to start at the top, with the records of the PCC and PCY, especially if you are looking for a will before about 1800 and suspect that the man concerned was reasonably well off. Wills in the PCC go back as far as the late 14th century, though they are more likely to be missing up to the late 17th cen-

tury. Wills proved in the PCC are now in the PRO, and those proved in the PCY are in the Borthwick Institute of Historical Research, York. Some of the yearly indexes to PCC wills are arranged in a rather curious way, on the basis of the first letter and the first vowel; thus, Clark – CA – comes before Cedric – CE. This takes a little getting used to.

Most wills proved in lower courts are now kept in the appropriate CRO, although some remain with Diocesan Record Offices, not all of which have been amalgamated with the CROs (remember, too, the boundaries of county and diocese are not always identical). To save time you can consult *Wills and Their Whereabouts* which gives lists of all locations and also of printed or microfilmed calendars and indexes. Many of the latter can be consulted in the library of the Society of Genealogists. When you have ascertained name and date, the institution concerned will probably be willing to conduct a search on your behalf and, if required, provide a copy of the will. See also the suggested sequence for a comprehensive search for a will in Don Steel's *Discovering Your Family History*.

For a period from the late 18th century, abstracts or copies of wills and admons were deposited at the Estate Duty Office. Registers of the abstracts are in the PRO. Most of the copies, when originals were known to exist, were recently destroyed, 'an almost unparalleled act of vandalism', writes Don Steel, 'approved by the Lord Chancellor and carried out despite the offer of the Society of Genealogists to house them.'

Do not neglect printed sources. A surprisingly large number of wills have been listed by local historical societies and other bodies. The local library will be able to bring them to your attention.

Welsh wills before 1858 are kept in the National Library of Wales, Aberystwyth, whilst later ones, as explained, are kept in the Principal Probate Registry, Somerset House. Scottish wills, or testaments as they should be called north of the border, before 1823 are in the Scottish Records Office, Old Register House, Edinburgh. Subsequently, they may be at either the Scottish Record Office or still held by the local Sheriff's court. They are usually accompanied by inventories, listing possessions room by room, from which you can practically reconstruct your ancestor's living conditions. Ireland is rather more complicated, and many wills were lost in the Dublin fire of 1922. The PRO in Dublin still has a large number, however, dating from the early 18th century. Northern Ireland wills since 1858 are in the Belfast PRO, which also has indexes of earlier wills, though the wills themselves may no longer exist. Ireland altogether tends to be something of a genealogical jungle, but the staff of the National Library in Dublin are always sympathetic towards serious inquiries.

Printed Sources

Your search for your ancestors will probably involve you in a good deal of reading sooner or later. If you turn up an officer in the Duke of Wellington's army, you will want to read as much as possible about the Peninsula War, especially the accounts of participants, of which there are a surprisingly large number (perhaps your ancestor wrote one of them!). If you discover a man who was a stage-coach proprietor, you will probably be visiting the library to seek copies of the works of Surtees and Nimrod and other reporters of the times to find out what his life was like. If your ancestor was a brewer, you will want to read about the brewing trade at the time he was engaged in it. It is obviously a great advantage to know something about the history of your ancestor's country, especially social and economic history. Most people who are sufficiently interested in the past to set out on the search for their own antecedents probably have a fair historical background already, but if you are a little weak on subjects such as the Corn Laws or the Enclosure movement, perhaps you need a quick refresher course. If you are comparatively ignorant of history generally, you are likely to miss the significance of some of the facts you discover, and you will not be able to exercise your imagination as constructively as you would if you were familiar with the larger historical context. Some people, it is true, live out their lives apparently unaffected by great national events (the absence of any mention of the Napoleonic wars from the novels of Jane Austen has often been remarked), but often the behaviour of individuals is governed by wars, plagues and other calamitous events or, equally, by sudden good fortune. The Napoleonic wars may have meant death for your ancestor if he were a military man, but if he were a corn chandler they may have meant great profit.

Apart from this indirect information or background material, books and other printed matter may give you some direct facts about your ancestors. The importance of making sure that no previous history of your family already exists has been mentioned in Chapter 1, and careful investigation of the catalogue of the British Library and other big libraries could save much time-consuming research for original sources in obscure archives. For help in locating such material you should consult the works of M. J. Kaminkow: *Genealogical Manuscripts and British Libraries* (1967) and *Genealogies in the Library of Congress: A Bibliography* (1972), with later supplements.

Many people begin their search for their ancestors in the belief, or at any rate the hope, that they have connections with the landed gentry if not the aristocracy. This is not necessarily mere snobbery: if you hope to trace your family farther back than the beginning of the 18th century, such a connection will be useful if not essential. Whether you have any evidence or not, it is not unlikely that you will find landowners or even a title of nobility among your ancestors, though obviously the chances of direct descent are less. There has been a good deal of movement up and down the social scale in the past two hundred years, and the conviction of some utterly unpretentious soul that he or she is the descendant of great lords and ladies is not always as silly as it may seem. The majority of titled people today sprang from humble origins quite recently, and the number of untitled people alive today who are descended from noble ancestors is certainly very much larger.

If you do discover a link with the peerage, then your task, or part of it, becomes fairly straightforward, since the peerage (discounting the modern innovation of life peers) is by nature hereditary. There is no problem in following the line back to the original creation of the peerage; two of the most useful printed sources for this are *Burke's Peerage* and *Debrett's Peerage*, still going strong despite the

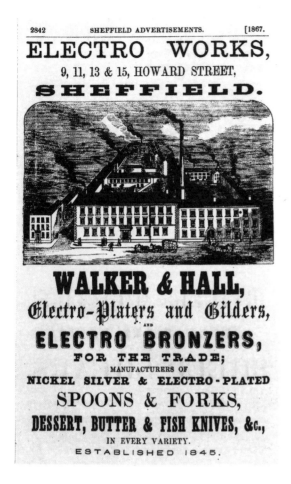

Directories, guides, newspapers and similar publications often contain advertisements of tradesmen with goods or services to offer. This Post Office directory of 1867 carries the address and business details of Walker and Hall, manufacturers of electro-plated cutlery in Sheffield.

pressures of egalitarianism. *Debrett's* has the grander reputation, but in fact *Burke's* is more useful from the genealogical point of view, although the manner in which the facts are set out, actually a triumph of concision and space-saving, takes a little time to master. *Burke's Landed Gentry* is equally useful for the squirearchy. The second edition, published in three volumes in 1846–49, with an index running to over 300 pages, is probably the best. It was then entitled *The Landed Gentry of Great Britain and Ireland*, but in 1899 *The Landed Gentry of Ireland* appeared separately.

If you had an ancestor who achieved some eminence, apart from being born to an eminent family, he may be in the *Dictionary of National Biography*. This great work includes many people of comparatively modest attainments, especially in

the professional or literary fields, although it also fails to include some who seem more worthy of posterity's attention. Since 1897 *Who's Who* has provided wider coverage, especially in those areas where the editors of the *Dictionary of National Biography* were somewhat dilatory, and the posthumous compilation *Who Was Who*, published at intervals, is easier to consult than the annual volumes of *Who's Who*. Another work, *Modern English Biography*, edited by Frederick Boase, is particularly useful for the second half of the 19th century.

Besides these general biographical works, there are a great number of similar reference books on particular professions. Many of them are of little use genealogically as they are confined to relatively recent times, but others, notably works on certain types of artists and craftsmen, show evidence of remarkable research in an earlier period. If you know the business of your ancestors you should certainly check the reference library for any books of this kind which might include him.

Directories tend to be of greater value, largely because they were first compiled at an early date. The first London directory was published over three hundred years ago, whilst most large towns had their own directories before the end of the 18th century. The early directories are usually confined to tradespeople and officials, but some include private citizens as well. Besides listing individuals, they often give a brief account of the district – local industries, schools, transport, and so on. The available directories are listed in *The London Directories 1677–1855* by C. W. F. Goss (1932), or *Guide to National and Provincial Directories of England and Wales* by J. E. Norton (1956). The largest collection of them is in the Guildhall Library (it includes many non-London directories), but the local reference library or CRO will probably have most of the directories for their areas.

The addresses given in old directories, and in other sources for that matter, can sometimes mislead. Nowadays everyone has a fixed, precise – and concise – address: number of house and name of street followed by district or town. But this system dates only from the last century with the introduction of an inexpensive and efficient postal service. In earlier times, when a man was asked where he lived he did not reply, 'No. 2, Avenue Road', but something like 'by the mill' or 'near the sign of the clockmaker'. (Lady Paston, in the 15th century, addressing a letter to her husband absent on business, wrote on it, 'To Thomas Greene, goodman of the George, by Powles Wharf, or to his wife, to send to Sir John Paston, wheresoever he be, at Calais, London, or other places'.) It is thus often hard to say exactly where someone lived in former times, even if there has been no reconstruction in the area. Even in the Victorian age, and occasionally later, no great reliance can be placed on addresses because house numbers, though common by that time, could change. When you find a record of a family living at two different numbers, or even in apparently different streets, it does not necessarily mean that the family had moved house between the two dates.

Another minor point to keep in mind when using a directory is that the information is not right up to date, and usually corresponds to the situation a year earlier than the date of publication of the directory. Thus, an address as given in, for example, the Census of 1861, is (or should be) correct for that year, but an address in a local directory of the same date is likely to be correct for the previous year. The lapse in time between compilation and publication, though in general rather shorter in the 19th century than today, is easily overlooked. For example, Gibbon is quoted as having written his *History of the Decline and Fall of the Roman Empire* in 1776, though of course that was the date when the first volume was published; Gibbon actually wrote some time earlier than that.

Books on local history have already been mentioned and you should have investigated this field when you discovered where your ancestors lived. Much depends on chance: some very good books have been written about quite small places, while other, much larger places have not so far been blessed with a really adequate chronicler. Such works, though invaluable for background knowledge, are not likely to be of any specific genealogical assistance unless your ancestor happened to be a substantial property owner or a figure of some local importance.

Undoubtedly, the greatest single enterprise in the area of local history is the *Victoria County History*, begun, as the name suggests, in the reign of Queen Victoria and to be found in almost all reference libraries. Unfortunately, it is still a long way from completion, but it is an unrivalled source of reference for the counties which have been completed, tracing the history of every manor and every parish from the earliest times. Some counties have other, earlier histories which contain information not to be found anywhere else. These books are often rare, but the local library will probably have a copy.

Old newspapers and periodicals can be valuable sources, although unless you know exactly where to look the sheer volume of print can seem overwhelming. Fortunately, the *Times* of London is indexed, but the majority of newspapers are not.

The monthly *Gentleman's Magazine* is especially useful for genealogy. From its first publication in 1731 up to 1868, it printed notices of births and – more often – marriages and deaths, mainly, of course, among the gentry but included an increasing number of fairly ordinary middle-class folk. Notable people received informative obituaries, while marriage notices often included a mention of such interesting items as the size of the bride's dowry. Elevated gossip of this kind is often fruitful, though not always reliable. Although there is a cumulative index of names for the *Gentleman's Magazine*, only surnames are listed, and if the surname is a common one a longish search may still be necessary. Since the more comprehensive index of births compiled by the Mormons became available, the *Gentleman's Magazine* is less used.

There are various other indexes of obituaries in the 18th century, published by bodies such as the Harleian Society, and drawn from other sources besides the *Gentleman's Magazine*. The fullest obituaries usually appeared in local newspapers, and it is often possible to track these down from an entry in one of the more general sources.

The largest collection of 19th- and 20th-century newspapers in Britain, despite losses suffered during the Second World War, is held by the British Library's Colindale branch in North London. A day ticket is only needed for entry to the Newspaper Library, Colindale although it is necessary to have a full reader's ticket for the British Library Reading Room in the British Museum.

If you do not know exactly what you are looking for, you may be able to save yourself unnecessary frustration by consulting the local reference library, the CRO or even the current successor of the newspaper concerned. Librarians are nearly always helpful, and a personal visit to the library is an advantage. However, often you can find out what you want to know by mail or telephone; many public libraries these days incorporate an information centre, and it is surprising what a variety of information they will provide. Always remember, when your task seems hopeless, that a host of professional people as well as well-informed amateurs are not only ready but genuinely willing to help. Sometimes, those whose help you enlist can become almost as interested in your quest as you are yourself. Therefore, do not be afraid of asking for advice or explaining exactly what you are hoping to accomplish.

Emigrants

Even before the Industrial Revolution, people moved about more often than is generally assumed, although as a rule they did not move very far. At different periods, large numbers of British subjects migrated to other lands, while foreigners also settled here. If you manage to trace your forbears back for two hundred years or more, there is a better than evens chance that you will find at least one immigrant among them. It is true, for instance, that the majority of British subjects today who are of West Indian or African descent arrived in Britain quite recently, but in fact there was also a sizeable number of blacks in England in the 18th century. It is often said of the United States that the population is a national melting pot, but to some extent this is also true of Britain and many other nations.

North America has certainly absorbed a large number of immigrants, especially European immigrants, than any other part of the world, while the British have scattered themselves more widely across the globe than any other people besides the Jews. The reason for this British mobility is obvious enough – colonies. The first English colonies overseas were founded before the beginning of the 17th century. By the end of the 19th not only had former English colonies evolved into new and independent nations, but the British had replaced them with a new empire in Africa and Asia. During the 17th century, about 250,000 people emigrated to North America from England. This is a considerable number when we remember that the population of England and Wales at the end of the century was only about 5,000,000. However, this was a mere trickle compared with later figures. It has been estimated that between 1770 and 1890 British immigrants to North America approached 12,000,000, while for Europe as a whole, annual overseas emigration in the period before the First

World War amounted to about 1,500,000.

There are, therefore, many people in North America and the former British dominions particularly, who if they hope to trace their ancestors back for any considerable distance must seek the evidence in the British Isles. But before they do that, they should, of course, discover as much as they can about their family in their own country. Even if you already know something concrete about your ancestors before they emigrated, it is still advisable to follow the general rule – work backwards one step at a time. There may be cases when it is possible and even quicker to work forwards from a known ancestor, but they are exceptional.

The importance of thorough research in your own country cannot be overemphasised. Nothing could be more annoying than to find your search blocked in England for lack of information which you could have acquired before you left home.

As a rule, the less mobile your ancestors were, the easier it is to trace them. Obviously, emigration or immigration poses special problems, but there is at least one advantage. An emigrant from one country is naturally an immigrant to another country, and the patchy, sparse character of records of migrants is to some extent compensated for by the fact that if his departure cannot be traced, maybe his arrival can, and vice versa.

If your ancestors were famous, then you will probably have little trouble in locating their movements. Indeed, the job may have been done already. We now know, for example, more about George Washington's antecedents than he did: his great-grandfather emigrated to Virginia in 1657, earlier forbears were described as 'gentlemen' and, earlier still, received land from King Henry VIII; several members of the family held minor offices under the Crown, and there was a family estate at

Old photographs are nearly always interesting and can provide some useful genealogical information. This shows three generations of a family of immigrants in Coburg, Nebraska in about 1887–8. The initials P.O. probably mean that the house is Coburg's Post Office.

Sulgrave, Northamptonshire. This much we know as a result of the interest which Washington's origins naturally arouse, but even so, it is significant that, although he came from a fairly prosperous and locally prominent family, we still do not know a great deal. To avoid disappointment, you should be aware that to trace the person who was responsible for your being an American or an Australian rather than a British subject, you will need some luck, especially if the migration took place more than one hundred years ago.

If you do not know either the date on which your ancestor(s) emigrated or their place of origin in the British Isles, and if your family name is a common one, it might be wiser to forget the whole business. In those circumstances the task is not impossible but the search is likely to be almost endless, with no assurance of positive results.

The crucial fact is the place of origin. If you know that, you are at least on equal terms with those whose families remained permanently in the country. Death certificates, which may provide in-

direct evidence of the date of emigration, also often indicate the place of birth. The same valuable facts can be gleaned from naturalization papers and similar documents (there are indexes to these records in the Library of Congress, Washington, D.C.). A great deal of work has been done on the early settlers in North America; you can find out more by consulting a book such as the *Topographical Dictionary of 2885 English Emigrants to New England 1620–1650* by C. E. Banks and E. E. Brownell (1957).

The obvious place to start looking for a migratory ancestor, providing you have some idea of the date he emigrated, is in ships' passenger lists. Unfortunately, there are huge gaps in these records, so you will first need to find out whether they exist for the period in which you are searching. There are, again, books that will help, notably *Original Lists of Persons Emigrating to America 1600–1700* by J. C. Hotton (1874), and *A Bibliography of Ship Passenger Lists 1538–1825* by A. H. Lancour (1966). Many of the original lists can be inspected in the PRO at Kew in south-west London. They usually give name, age and occupation and, sometimes, place of origin. There are, however, large gaps up until 1890, when regular lists of passengers in ships leaving British ports began to be kept; they are also in the PRO at Kew, and they are arranged annually by port and date of sailing. As long as you do not have too inconveniently long a time span to cover, the search should not be too difficult. Although you may not be able to find the place of origin, you will have enough information to carry your search a step further. It is likely, however, that you are concerned with an earlier date than 1890, in which case you must search among less comprehensive records. The National Archives in Washington contain lists of passengers arriving in U.S. ports from 1835 onwards, though there are some gaps and no places of origin. After 1892, when the immigration bureau was established on Ellis Island in New York Harbour, the records are much fuller, but that again is probably too late a date.

The 18th century is particularly difficult, an unfortunate fire having destroyed what would have been a most valuable record. At that period details of emigrants leaving England were recorded by Customs officials at the port of embarkation. Early in the 19th century these returns, which normally listed place of residence as well as age and trade, were sent to be stored centrally in the Custom House in London but, alas, all perished when the Custom House was destroyed by fire in 1814.

If you have no clue to the date of your ancestors' emigration, there are several alternative courses to follow. If the surname is a very uncommon one, you may be able to track it down to a particular district; *Homes of Family Names in Great Britain* by H. B. Guppy (1890), will assist you. Slightly more promising is the possible existence of a will. You could, for example, search the printed index to PCC wills for the approximate period in the hope of finding another member of the family. It must be admitted that this too is something of a forlorn hope. The farther back in time you have to go, the more difficult it becomes; once you get back into the 17th century you will probably need a large amount of luck somewhere. The extreme difficulty of tracing family descent back to the early period explains why such an improbably large number of people today are able to claim, without fear of denial, that their ancestors came over in the *Mayflower*. Early immigrants to North America, up to about 1630, were granted a royal licence to leave the country; later, similar licences were sometimes issued by government officials. Unfortunately, very few have been preserved; those that have are listed in *Original Lists of Person's Emigrating to America 1600–1700*.

Although, in general, it is easier to trace your ancestors if they were fairly prosperous or prominent people, the chances of tracing emigrants may be rather better if they were impoverished nobodies. There are in the PRO certain lists of people who travelled to the colonies by some kind of assisted-passage scheme; for example, those who departed for North America involuntarily under the 1662 Act for the Relief of the Poor. Colonies like the Cape of Good Hope and New Zealand were originally settled very largely by state-assisted immigrants, the costs being recouped by land sales in the colonies concerned.

If your ancestor went to North America as an indentured servant, there must have been some form of written contract. If this still exists it will give many personal details, including place of departure in Britain and place of arrival in the West Indies or the American colonies. These indentures are held either at the Corporation of London Records Office, or among the Treasury papers at the PRO; some are indexed by name. If you know (or suspect) that your ancestor arrived as an indentured servant, but cannot find further details of him, you may be able to trace his origin through his master (assuming you can find out who *he* was). The latter, if he too was a recent immigrant, was likely to recruit servants from his own former neighbourhood. You are, therefore, more likely to be able, perhaps through a will, to trace such a man's original home than the home of a servant.

In some colonies, the death certificate of a recent settler mentions his length of residence in the colony, and from that you can deduce the date of his passage.

There are a number of other avenues to explore in seeking migrant ancestors. For example, many settlers in the American and other colonies received land grants from the Crown. Indexes of these are kept in the Library of Congress, which also has copies of many of the documents concerned. Many of the originals will still be found in county courthouses. They may not be of much direct help, but they will probably offer some guidance as to where you should search next.

Irish emigrants to the United States and Canada waiting to board ship at Cork.

Trades and Professions

As a rule, the occupation of your forbears is one of the first things you learn about them. If you do not know it already, your research at the GRO will probably have apprised you of it, as it is generally given on marriage or death certificates. This opens up large new areas for research, which you will naturally wish to enter because, even if they offer no substantial advance in your genealogical studies, your ancestors' trade is bound to be of great interest. The members of certain professions and trades are much better documented than others, but you can usually find out something about even the most unpromising occupations. In some cases you may be able to find out a great deal.

The Services

An army, said Napoleon, marches on its stomach, but many people who have served in the army since have felt that what really keeps it going is a vast quantity of paper. This predilection for paperwork is a great nuisance to those who have to compile it, no doubt, but it is often a great joy to historians and genealogists. The records are, naturally, fewer as you go back in time, though there is a surprising quantity of material for quite early times. In general, officers are much better documented than other ranks.

For officers in the Royal Navy, there are a number of printed biographies giving details of their career and, sometimes, their parents and other relations, especially if the latter also have naval connections. The outstanding example is probably W. R. O'Byrne's *Naval Biographical Dictionary* (1849), which includes every living naval officer of the rank of lieutenant and above – about 5,000 of them – for the year 1845.

The Admiralty records, which are now in the PRO, are intimidatingly massive. Before you plunge in you would do well to consult the relevant section of the PRO Guide. The *Navy Lists* date from the 18th century and give the names of serving officers by rank and seniority. Successive lists will demonstrate how your naval ancestor's career progressed. A list of *Commissioned Sea Officers of the Royal Navy from 1660 to 1815* was published by the National Maritime Museum in 1954, and as this is more accessible, you might consult it first. It is possible, however, that the *Navy Lists* will not get you very much further. Perhaps more useful are the passing certificates of naval lieutenants, dating mostly from the late 18th century, which give details of the previous career and very often have a birth certificate attached as proof that the candidate had passed his twentieth birthday. Incidentally, too much reliance should not be placed on the recorded births in the armed services without supporting evidence. According to naval history, a midshipman appearing for his lieutenant examination could get a false birth certificate made by forgers waiting outside the Navy Office. The ages given by officers are certainly unreliable; Nelson is one of the best-known examples of a man who gave a false age to the naval authorities. Nevertheless, the passing certificates can be informative. They are indexed for some years only; otherwise it is necessary to check each volume. There are also passing certificates for some other ranks, such as boatswain, but in general ordinary seamen are not well documented before the mid-19th century; they were essentially part-timers, hired and fired according to the need of the moment.

Without wishing any ill fortune to your naval ancestor, there is no doubt that the chances of tracing him are better if he was at some time involved in some catastrophe: for example, seriously wounded or court-martialled for mutiny. Among

Service records give some details unlikely to be found in any other source (such as the colour of eyes and hair). This certificate records that Edward Oliver signed on for ten years' service, though his record of service shows that he served a longer period. *Adm. 139/256.*

Records of court martials also usually include details of the accused's previous career. Ship's musters, some going back to the 18th century and earlier, are helpful if you know on what ship a man served. For ratings, besides name and rank, they usually give age, place of birth and whether the man was press-ganged or not. If you know where a man was at a certain date but not the ship on which he served, you can find out the name of the ship by consulting the List Books, which go back to the reign of Charles II.

There are other collections of documents which may prove useful; in fact, if you had an ancestor in the Navy, there is almost certainly a mention of him somewhere in the Admiralty records, especially since the 18th century. The problem is to find out where it is. The earlier the period, the more difficult the search; many of the earlier records are not indexed, or at any rate not reliably indexed. Much depends on the amount of time available for research, on the skill of the researcher and, indeed, on luck. For example, there are many large bundles of captains' letters, grouped chronologically and then alphabetically under the officer's name. Even if your ancestor was not a captain, there may well be a reference to him somewhere in these documents, but it would hardly be worth investigating unless you had some special reason to think his name might crop up in a particular place. (The custom of a young officer or midshipman serving in a ship whose captain was a relative, perhaps an uncle, sometimes suggests a possible discovery among the captains' letters.) Many collections of documents of this kind in the PRO have not yet been fully exploited by the numerous professional historians who specialise in naval history. It is, therefore, perhaps unrealistic to expect amateur researchers to make a thorough search among them.

The records of the Royal Marines are also in the PRO. Although some of them have been lost, enlistment or attestation forms – name, age, birthplace, trade and other details – go back to 1790. Ideally, you need to know the date of attestation or of discharge. If you do not, you will find the alphabetically arranged description books easier to use. The registers of service are even better, but they start only in 1842.

Army records are no less extensive than naval ones, and their qualities, both good and bad, are similar. It is again easier to trace officers than other ranks, but the regimental system presents what is usually an advantage, to genealogical researchers. Some records of individual regiments are held locally in Army record offices, regimental museums, etc., while the regimental records of births, marriages and deaths are in the GRO. However, the great bulk of the Army's records, like the Navy's,

the Admiralty records are registers of pensions and other payments made to wounded sailors and to the widows of sailors killed in action. The amount of useful information they contain is variable, but they frequently note personal details not easily ascertained from other sources. From 1737 the naval hospital at Greenwich (founded as the equivalent of the Chelsea hospital for soldiers) kept registers of the pensioners it admitted. The genealogist Gerald Hamilton-Edwards discovered in his own family a petition written in 1810 to the Prince Regent from one of his forbears. It was an application for a pension as compensation for an accident suffered during the course of duty, which resulted in his being invalided from his ship. The document included an account of Lieutenant Edward's naval career as well as giving his current address.

Edward Oliver.   No. 25529.

No. on Ship's Books	Date of Badge	Seaman Gunner's Certificate	Character	Ship	Age	Entry	Rating	Discharge	Cause of Discharge	Time of Service Years of 365 Days	Days
S.C. 16.				Centaur	29.	24 Feb. 55.	Stoker	3 Feb. 58.	D.D.C.J	2	183 / 163
				"		4 Feb. 58.	Lg. Stoker	5 Aug. 58.		—	183
S.C. C.S.25529 1 June 55 10 yo.			Good.	"		6 Aug. 58.	Stoker	17 Nov. 58.			
317.			Good.	Hannibal		18 Nov. 58.	"	11 Jan. 59.			
19.			Good.	Pigmy		12 Jan. 59.	"	31 Dec. 61.	Transferred to		313
48.			V. Good.	"		1 Jan. 62.	"	31 Dec. 63.			
1263.			V. Good.	Asia		1 Jan. 64.	"	22 Jan. 64.			
198.			Good.	Hector		23 Jan. 64.	"	12 June 65.	Shore.		1116
341.				Valorous		7 Feb. 67.	"	2 July 67.		—	
147.			V. Good.	"		3 July 67.	Lg. Stoker	13 Sep. 67.			
858.			V. Good.	Asia		14 Sep. 67.	"	29 Nov. 67.		2	125

List of ships on which Edward Oliver served between 1855 and 1867. *Adm. 139/256.*

is in the PRO. Consult *Tracing Your Ancestors in the PRO* and the PRO guide, where the holdings are briefly described.

Among printed books, there are no great biographical compendia of army officers to compare with O'Byrne's work for the early Victorian Navy. But there are many regimental histories, of varying standards, as well as such resources as Sir John Fortescue's famous *History of the British Army* in thirteen volumes (1899–1930). There is, moreover, a very good modern book, *In Search of Army Ancestry* by Gerald Hamilton-Edwards (1977), which should certainly be among your preparatory reading if your ancestors were military men.

It is not difficult to trace an officer's career through the printed *Army Lists* from the late 18th century onwards, from which period the lists are printed and indexed. Printed lists actually go back somewhat earlier, and there are some manuscript lists as early as 1702. Most of the printed lists are available at other places besides the PRO, for example the National Army Museum and the Society of Genealogists. Through the successive volumes you can follow your military forbear until the point when he sold his commission or was killed in action or died.

Another fruitful source of information about army officers is the Commander-in-Chief's Memoranda, from 1793. They deal with applications for commissions and include letters from influential persons in support of the application, which may contain much personal information about him that

is not to be found in the *Army Lists*. The Half-Pay Warrants may record the death date of an officer on half pay and the names of his executors. From that you may be able to trace his will, which in most cases will have been proved in the PCC. It is much easier to trace an officer after about 1829, when returns were made of all serving officers; these normally include records of age, marriage and children as well as career record.

To trace a soldier of non-commissioned rank, the crucial factor (unless he lived in comparatively recent times) is his regiment. The Station Returns record the whereabouts of every regiment at any time. If you know where your ancestor was stationed at a particular date you can at least narrow down the choice of regiments to a reasonable number, and perhaps identify the actual regiment to which he belonged. If you cannot locate him in this way, you must try to establish his regiment by other means. Since you know already that he was in the army, you will almost certainly have some clue, if not to his actual regiment, then to some place in which he served or some battle in which he fought, knowledge that can lead you to the correct regiment. Failing even that, you may be able to hazard an intelligent guess; if he came from Norfolk, for instance, the Royal Norfolk Regiment would be an obvious choice. Should this last resort also fail, your search is, for all practical purposes, blocked. But you will have other lines to follow, and sooner or later they may lead you to the evidence you need.

Of course, unless you are a military history buff, you may not know much about British regiments in the first place; their history is somewhat complicated by dissolutions and mergers, which have affected even some of the most famous regiments in recent times. Arthur Swinson's *A Register of the Regiments and Corps of the British Army*, 1972, is a good guide. If, for example, the only clue to your ancestor's regiment is a reference in an old diary to some regimental nickname, Swinson's book will identify the regiment indicated. Your next step would probably be to read an individual regimental history.

The chief documentary sources since about the middle of the 18th century (earlier, the records are rather sparse) are the regimental muster books along with the attestation and discharge papers. The muster rolls are arranged by rank and, besides name and rank, they give the date of enlistment. They may also give the age, place of birth, trade and, from 1868, wife and children of the soldier. Attestation and discharge papers and description books, if available, give more details, including the man's health and conduct record and a physical description. As Gerald Hamilton-Edwards has written, 'it is quite a remarkable thing that you may be able to discover the colour of your ancestor's eyes and hair, an ancestor who was serving perhaps at Waterloo as a private soldier.'

As with the Navy, there is a multitude of subsidiary records of various kinds: widows' pension applications, casualty returns, registers of Chelsea hospital (for army pensioners, whose uniforms are still a decorative feature of London), arrest warrants for deserters, and many more.

It is not very likely that you will need to consult the service record of an ancestor in the Royal Air Force, since the junior service was founded as recently as 1918. However, if you should, the R.A.F. Association will be able to help.

The Clergy

As you would expect, since they were once in charge of the business of keeping registers, the clergy are well documented; you should be able to find out some information about clerical ancestors from printed records alone. Crockford's *Clerical Dictionary*, a 'Who's Who' of the Church of England, was first published in 1858 and any ordained clergyman living then or since will be found listed therein. The *Index Ecclesiasticum* was originally intended to include 'all Ecclesiastical Dignitaries in England and Wales since the Reformation'. It never achieved that ambitious aim; however it does cover the period 1800–1840. There are various other lists of clergy, such as the Fawcett Index at the Society of Genealogists, which is useful for clergy in the North of England and Scotland.

Since clergymen up to the mid-19th century were almost always university graduates, one obvious place to look for them is in the printed records of the universities. Until the 19th century there were only two, Oxford and Cambridge, in England, so this is not very difficult. The matriculation registers (*Alumni Oxoniensis*) and university records of Oxford usually give the father's name and place of residence, and sometimes, especially for clergy in the later period, some additional personal details. The Cambridge registers are, on the whole, more informative than the Oxford equivalents. It is often possible to trace several generations of a family through the university registers.

Other records of Church of England clergy can be found in the appropriate Diocesan Record Office (now usually amalgamated with the equivalent CRO). They include, for example, certificates of ordination, often with baptism certificates attached, as well as a variety of documents less easy to exploit unless you happen to know exactly what you are looking for.

It is more difficult to trace ministers of other religions or denominations, unless they lived comparatively recently. Roman Catholic priests after the Reformation often had to maintain a secret existence, and practised their religion under various forms of restraint until the 19th century. There are printed biographical dictionaries of some Roman Catholic orders, such as the Benedictines, and the Catholic Record Society has published much material of genealogical interest. Otherwise, in the case of a Roman Catholic priest or a Non-Conformist minister, you would do best to contact the headquarters of the church or group concerned; institutions like the Methodists' Archives and Research Centre are always sympathetic to serious inquiries. Oddly enough, the situation is sometimes easier when seeking ministers of immigrant groups. As noted earlier, Jewish records tend to be both fuller and more carefully preserved than those of other minorities. The Jewish Historical Society is the body to approach. Its periodical *Transactions* contains many articles of interest, as do the *Proceedings* of the Huguenot Society, for French Protestant immigrants.

Ministers of the Presbyterian Church of Scotland can probably be found in the volumes of *Fasti Ecclesiae Scoticanae*, along with much information about their families, and in the Kirk Session Records in the Scottish Record Office, which are also useful for laymen.

Lawyers

If one of your ancestors was a lawyer in England or Wales, you must find out whether he was a barrister or a solicitor: barristers were admitted to practise at the bar through one of the inns of court; while a solicitor is not a member of the bar and does not appear as an advocate in the higher courts. Barristers are fairly easily traced through the records of the inns of court, many of whose registers of admissions have been published. Failing that, further inquiries can be made from the librarians of the inns. Judges are normally former barristers, and can therefore be traced in the same way, though as a rule a judge is a sufficiently eminent person to be recorded in more general sources, such as the *Dictionary of National Biography*.

Solicitors are a greater problem. In the past comparatively few of them attended university, so the university registers are unlikely to help. Providing you know some details of the man concerned, you may be able to trace his will (though not all solicitors, despite their urging others to do so, made a will themselves). The *Law Lists*, which go back to 1775, usually mention the death of a solicitor, as well as giving the district where he practised. An apprentice lawyer is 'articled' to a solicitor, and the records of these articles, going back to 1729, are kept in the PRO. For the early period they are divided between the Court of Common Pleas and the King's Bench. They are arranged chronologically by date of admission and there is an index. These articles can sometimes prove extra-valuable when, for example, it turns out – and it was fairly common – that the solicitor to whom your ancestor was articled was in fact a relative.

Magistrates or justices of the peace (J.P.) are laymen, and if you have an ancestor who was a J.P. you may find some record of him in the CRO. Local newspapers may also mention him, though it can be a long job to comb their files.

Doctors

Members of the medical profession were often university graduates and, if so, they can be traced through the registers of Oxford, Cambridge and other universities, especially Edinburgh, Leyden in Holland (at one time a favourite place for English medical students) and Trinity College, Dublin. The Royal College of Physicians, which was founded in 1518, retains records of some of its members, and many of the more eminent are listed in Monk's *Roll of the Royal College of Physicians*.

Before the 19th century medical men were generally of lower social status than they subsequently became; surgeons especially were hardly more than humble craftsmen, allied with barbers. The foundation of the Royal College of Surgeons in 1800 indicated their rising status, and if your ancestor was an F.R.C.S. the College will probably have some record of him.

Other records of medical men of different kinds may be found in the Diocesan Record Office, since at one time they had to be licensed to practise by the local archdeacon's court, or among the records of the Society of Apothecaries in the Guildhall, London. The latter, from the late 18th century onwards, are quite detailed.

Other Professionals

The materials for researching professional people in general are large and varied, and cannot be summarised here in any detail. There are two obvious places to start. Most professions have some kind of association which is, at least partly, concerned with the history of the profession and its practitioners, and frequently holds registers of former members as well as other historical records. For example, if you are looking for an architect, you would hope to find out something about him from the Royal Institute of British Architects. Secondly, there are printed works of reference, not always exclusively biographical, for a great number of professions. You may well find your architect in the *Biographical Dictionary of English Architects 1660–1840* by H. M. Colvin. In the arts especially, there are famous works like *Grove's Dictionary of Music and Musicians* (do not be content to consult only the edition in your local library, which is probably the latest, as it is possible you may have better luck with an earlier edition). But there are also many comparatively obscure works on more limited subjects, like 18th-century watercolourists or 19th-century silhouettists, etc., books which, though seldom removed from the dusty upper shelves of the reference library, occasionally prove to be exactly the source you are hoping to find.

Tradesmen

The humbler the occupation in which your ancestor was engaged, the harder it is, as a rule, to find a record of him at work. Nevertheless, there are obvious sources for tradesmen of various kinds.

Local directories and newspapers have already been mentioned. If your ancestor was engaged in what is nowadays called a service industry, he may have advertised his service in the press. He may have had printed trade cards, of which there is a substantial collection in the Guildhall Library, London (this collection relates to London only), or trade tokens, of which there are published catalogues. In rural areas particularly, bills and receipts from local tradesmen often turn up among the archives of local institutions and rich families.

An important source for tradesmen is the guild or company, a form of association often, though inaccurately, regarded as a kind of early prototype of a trade union. Guilds controlled the economic life of the nation at local level to a considerable extent from the 12th century onwards. They tended to be conservative institutions, largely preoccupied with preserving the status of their own members; although you will not find any as early as the 12th century, their records are, on the whole, carefully preserved. There are published histories of many of the great City Companies of London, though the guilds in general are not so well represented in modern historiography as one might expect. In London, research into the records begins, naturally enough, at the Guildhall. Provincial guildhalls also hold some records, though you should probably begin with the CRO.

If you have an ancestor who is known to have been a freeman of the City of London, it is possible to find out what his trade was, or at least the Company he belonged to, by writing to the Corporation of London Records Office, where the registers of freemen, to the year 1915, can be found. Records of freemen of the provincial boroughs can be located through the town clerk or through the local library.

A great deal of research is going on continuously into the crafts and craftsmen of the past. Much of it is published, but often in obscure publications; it can be easily overlooked if it occurs only in some learned journal, or perhaps in an unpublished Ph.D. thesis. However, if you have learned as much as you reasonably can about the nature of the trade concerned in the period when your ancestor was a member of it, you will know where to look or whom to ask about extending your investigation to the less obvious sources. If your ancestor belonged to some especially interesting or high-class trade, such as that of goldsmith, there is a fair chance of tracing him, even if he was an obscure craftsman living in a provincial town two or three centuries ago.

In former times, the only practical way of learning a trade was by serving as an apprentice to a qualified craftsman. An Elizabethan act of parliament ordained a period of seven years apprenticeship, though later the period varied according to the trade. Many indentures or articles of apprenticeship have survived, and together they form perhaps the most valuable source of information about tradesmen. They usually give the name and address of the father as well as the master, among other facts. There are local registers which sometimes go back a very long way, and the London City Companies hold their own registers. Unfortunately, there was no central registration until 1710, when a tax was imposed on indentures based on the fee initially paid to the master. As a result, a centralised register of apprentices had to be kept; they are now in the PRO. The Society of Genealogists has an Apprentices Index (also an index of masters) covering most of the 18th century, which gives the vital information, so that it may not be necessary to consult the original registers in the PRO. In recent years much work has been done on apprenticeship indentures in provincial towns and cities, and, if available, can be obtained through the CRO.

There were some apprentices for whom, at one period, no premium, and therefore no tax, was paid. They included pauper children, apprenticed by the parish (like Oliver Twist), and records of them can often be found in the parish churchwardens' accounts, now probably in the local CRO.

Trade card of John Hardman and Co., metal workers in silver, brass and wrought iron, 19th-century. These are useful in tracing the address and details of a possible relative, especially if the card is in the possession of an old relation or is found in between the pages of a book which has long been in the family.

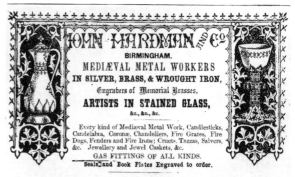

Property and Taxes

Manorial records are considerably older than parish registers, though they also continue into the 19th century. If you succeed in tracing your family back to the early 16th century, not in fact very likely unless your ancestors were people of some eminence, then manorial records may be your only source.

The manor was the ancient unit of land tenure, based on the estate of the lord of the manor. Sometimes it roughly coincided with the parish; when it did not, some manor and parish business often overlapped and in the course of time the parish came to supercede the manor in many respects. The manor was both a political and an economic unit: a local government district with the lord of the manor as the political head. His powers, though they varied from place to place, were considerable. The lesser inhabitants of the manor were in effect his subjects, and they were tied to him by a complex system of customary duties and obligations. The lord's jurisdiction was enforced by the manor court, the most vital and most complicated institution of the manor, presided over by the lord's steward and attended by all the tenants of the manor, some of whom also acted as a jury. Attendance was compulsory and the names of absentees, who had to pay a fine, were recorded in the minutes. From about the 15th century there were two types of manorial court, the Court Leet and the Court Baron. It was the latter which was usually concerned with land tenure and property rights, while the Court Leet dealt with election of officials and with crimes and misdemeanours, eventually becoming redundant as the county and parish authorities took over these functions. However, the two types of court were not always clearly distinguished; one often comes across the Court Baron conducting business which one would have expected to have fallen within the province of the Court Leet. By the 19th century all manorial courts were falling into disuse, and the necessary business was conducted less formally by the steward.

In their prime, the manorial courts had a much wider function than the modern concept of a 'court'. Criminal matters were dealt with, mostly petty crimes like assault and theft, and a large amount of business was taken up with breaches of manorial custom – someone failing to keep his pigs out of the common field or cutting wood on the lord's estate. They also dealt with such matters as marriage arrangements, transfer of land, civil suits, and so on. The manorial court rolls therefore often include information about quite humble individuals. In some parts of England it has proved possible to trace a family of villeins, or serfs, through several generations in the 13th or 14th centuries, via entries in the manorial records. Unfortunately, however, it is seldom possible to follow such families down to modern times.

If you *have* succeeded in tracing your ancestors back to the 16th century through the parish registers, then it is possible that manorial records will carry you back another two or three centuries, but do not put too much hope in it. The chances are that the records you seek have not survived at all, and even if they have, it is not always easy to trace them. Some are still in private hands. The Historical Manuscripts Commission keeps a register of manor court rolls, from which you can learn their location, but probably the best step initially is to inquire at the CRO, where the records may be deposited anyway.

These old records are also sometimes difficult to interpret; they are written in Latin up to 1732 and employ words not widely known today. However, manorial records, if they do exist, are not only virtually the sole source for the majority of people up to the 16th century, they are also often very detailed, giving more exact information than the parish registers.

The main business of the manorial courts, or at any rate the business in which we are most interested, was concerned with landholding, rentals, inheritance, etc. When a tenant died, a jury decided on the basis of manorial custom what his estate consisted of, who was his heir, and what 'fine' or heriot was due to the lord upon the new tenant's inheritance. If the deceased were a tenant at will (i.e. he was able to bequeath his property to whom he wished, as distinct from a customary tenant whose property descended automatically to his eldest son or to some other preordained relation), then the records would often include extracts from the dead man's will and perhaps deeds relating to the property.

Customary tenants were copyholders. The origin of copyhold tenure, which incidentally lasted into the 20th century, lay in the fact that the original tenants were villeins, who were granted land in exchange for working on the manorial demesne – the land farmed directly by the lord of the manor.

An extract from the General Register of Saisines for 1688–89. To read such documents one needs to have a knowledge of the Scots vernacular as well as contemporary handwriting. *Keeper of Records, Scotland. (R.S. 3/21).*

As time went on, labour services were increasingly commuted to a cash payment or 'quit rent'. In principle, all the possessions of the tenant reverted to the lord on the tenant's death, and after this practice had died out, the lord continued to levy a fine on the property when the heir succeeded to it. During the 16th century, landowners tended to raise these fines sharply to compensate for the declining value of money, for quit rents were fixed and therefore, in real terms, growing steadily smaller. As a result there were many actions in the Court of Chancery disputing the increased fines. Chancery proceedings are now in the PRO, Chancery Lane.

Records relating to landholding and property are in general numerous but patchy and complex. One of the most promising series of official deeds are the Feet of Fines, which are nearly complete for as far back as the 12th century. This was a means for transferring property by a formal legal dispute in which the holder of the land was technically sued by the legal owner, who agreed to accept a certain payment to allow the holder to remain in possession. Three copies of the agreement were made, one for each party and the third, or 'foot', to be enrolled in the Court of Common Pleas. The latter (now in the PRO) are often of special value to the genealogist because a man's children or heirs are often included. There are calendars to these enrollments, covering most of the 16th, 17th and 18th centuries, arranged by year, county, name and property.

Another form of conveyance, called Recoveries, involved a similar artificial legal dispute, which made it possible to release land entailed in the family. Deeds of this kind, like Feet of Fines, appear in the rolls of the Court of Common Pleas in the PRO.

Lease and Release deeds, a common method of transferring property between the reign of Elizabeth I and the reign of Victoria, are rather less valuable because, for one thing, there was no central registry of them. They were a means of circumventing expensive legal procedures resulting from feudal rights: following the lease of land, the rights of ownership were released; only the two parties involved held copies of the deeds. Along with other old types of lease, these have been collected by CROs, but they remain rather an elusive source.

Property deeds, though tiresome to read, can be very valuable, as they may reveal a whole series of family members. The registration of title to property began in the early 18th century, and is now centralised in the Land Registry. Current deeds may not go back very far, as today it is necessary to prove property title for fifty years only. The older deeds may still exist, but possibly in a quite different place.

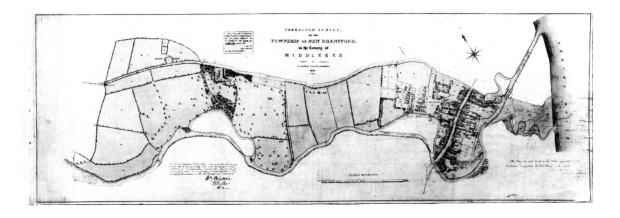

A tithe map of Brentford, Middlesex, 1838. These maps, which cover most of the kingdom, are an invaluable source. Each field is numbered, and they are accompanied by schedules giving the name of the field, its number on the map, its area and, of course, its proprietor. *IR 30/21/7.*

It is largely the lack of centralization which makes conveyancing – in principle a very fruitful area – so difficult to research. In Scotland, however, there are the Saisines Registers. *Saisine* is the same word as the English *seisin*, and refers to the ceremony of taking possession of property, usually involving the symbolic acceptance of a sample of earth or some such ritual. Thanks to the Saisines Registers, which run into thousands of bulky volumes, it is possible to trace the ownership of a piece of land in Scotland since the early 17th or, in a few cases, the end of the 16th century. For part of this period there are well-indexed abridgements which may contain all the information you need and are much easier to use. The Scottish Record Office will furnish the names of professional researchers who are experienced in working with the Saisines Registers as well as other property records like the Register of Deeds, which are more fully described in Hamilton-Edward's *In Search of Scottish Ancestry.*

It is often difficult to locate exactly where a piece of property lay, as what was once a farm is now all too likely to be covered by roads and buildings. Bethnal Green, as its name suggests, was a rural village in the 18th century, where Londoners went for weekend relaxation; while south of Islington, you passed through open fields on your way to the City. Old maps can often locate a building that no longer exists, or a farm long since swallowed up by the spreading town. Finding a detailed large-scale map of 18th-century or earlier date for a particular district is partly, of course, a matter of luck, though the 19th century seldom presents a problem. The most useful, or rather, most comprehensive maps are the Tithe maps compiled at the beginning of the Victorian period, which cover about 12,000 parishes. They show who owned the land and who occupied it, and the tithes that had to be paid for each plot. For earlier maps, you should enquire at the CRO.

The CROs also hold records of the awards of enclosures before the 19th century. Again, maps of enclosures are most numerous for the 19th century, though some go back to Tudor times, when the enclosure of common land for fields was already a source of social discontent. One of the greatest repositories of old maps is the Map Room of the British Museum, but for local maps the CRO is usually the best source.

Rate books, which go back to about the middle of the 18th century, are useful for locating addresses if you have had no luck with local directories. They give the name of each householder (who is not, of course, necessarily the owner of the house) and the rates payable on the property. They are normally to be found, with other parish records, at the CRO.

Rates are a form of tax, and all governments raise the income they require to meet national expenditure by taxation (including Customs and Excise duties). Income tax, which is nowadays by far the largest single source of government revenue, is a comparatively modern invention. In most countries it was introduced at some time in the 19th century as a means of raising revenue for extraordinary expenditure, such as war; governments usually assured the irate taxpayers that it was a temporary expedient only. (The income tax imposed by Sir Robert Peel in England in 1842 was levied at the rate of 7d (3p) in the £, but provoked fierce opposition nonetheless.) In the past, governments sometimes levied taxes similar to income tax, like the 14th-century poll tax, levied on every male subject over 14 years of age: some of the returns for this tax have been printed. Poll taxes were also raised on a number of occasions in the 17th century and the returns, if they still exist, sometimes give individual family relationships.

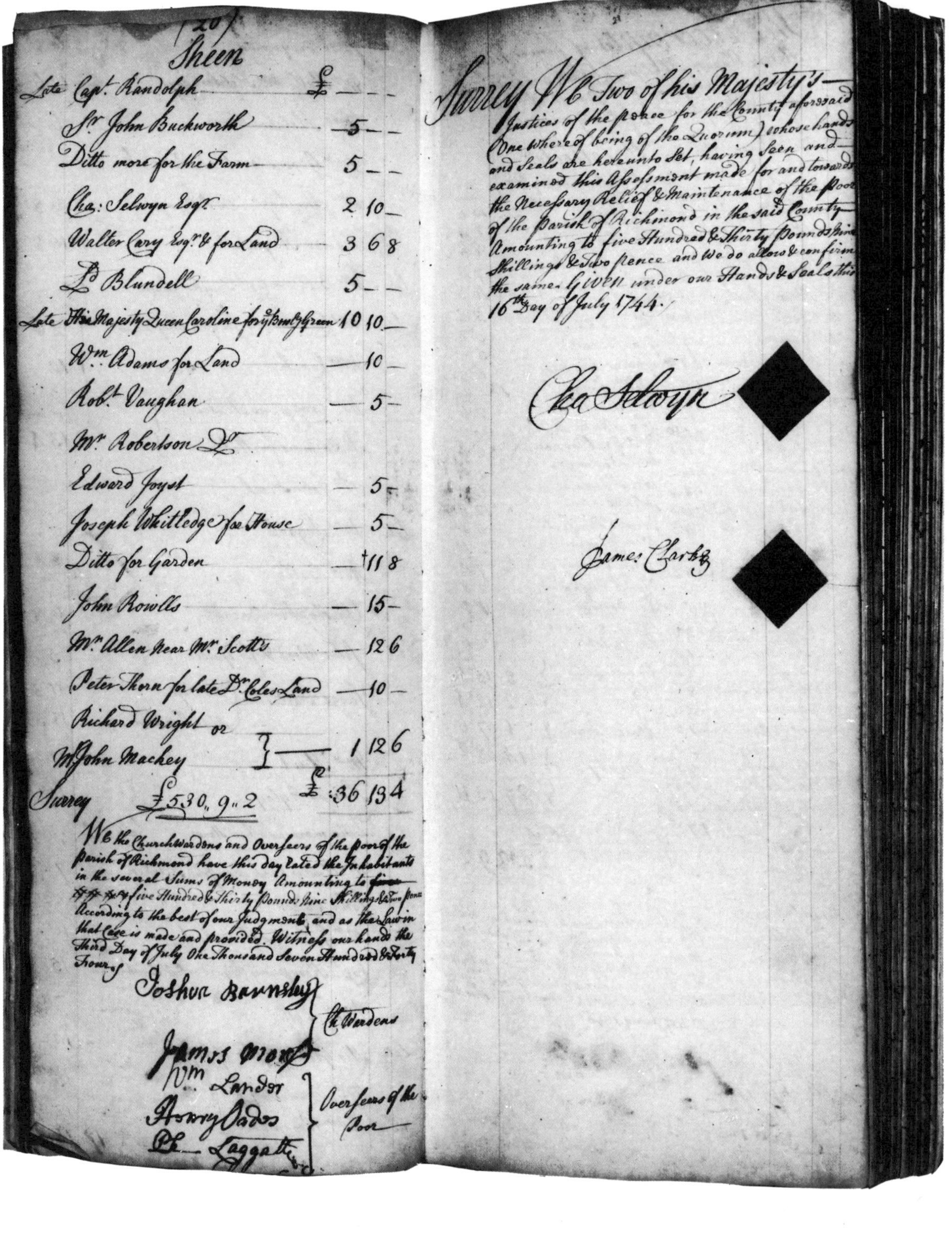

Sheen

	£	s	d
Late Capt. Randolph		—	—
Sr John Buckworth		5	—
Ditto more for the Farm		5	—
Cha: Selwyn Esqr	2	10	—
Walter Cary Esqr & for Land	3	6	8
Ld Blundell		5	—
Late His Majesty Queen Caroline for &c at Sheen	10	10	—
Wm Adams for Land		10	—
Robt Vaughan		5	—
Mr Robertson			
Edward Joyst		5	—
Joseph Whitledge for House		5	—
Ditto for Garden		11	8
John Rowlls		15	—
Mr Allen near Mr Scotts		12	6
Peter Thorn for late Dr Coles Land		10	—
Richard Wright or Mr John Mackey	1	12	6
Sheen	36	13	4

Surrey £ 530..9..2

WE the Churchwardens and Overseers of the poor of the parish of Richmond have this day rated the Inhabitants in the several Sums of Money Amounting to five Hundred & Thirty Pounds Nine Shillings & two pence According to the best of our judgment and as the Law in that Case is made and provided. Witness our hand the Third Day of July One Thousand Seven Hundred & forty four.

Joshua Barnsley } Ch. Wardens

James Mort
Wm Lander
Henry Oades
Richard Taggatt } Overseers of the poor

Surrey WE Two of his Majesty's Justices of the peace for the County aforesaid (One whereof being of the Quorum) whose hands and Seals are hereunto Set, having Seen and examined this Assessment made for and towards the Necessary Relief & Maintenance of the poor of the Parish of Richmond in the said County Amounting to five Hundred & Thirty Pounds Nine Shillings & Two pence and We do allow & confirm the same. Given under our Hands & Seals this 16th Day of July 1744.

Chas Selwyn

James Clerke

In general, taxation returns are in the PRO, though some are among local archives. One major source of revenue during the 18th and 19th centuries was the Land Tax, levied at 4 shillings (20p) in the £ during the reign of William III, when it first became a regular feature of the revenue. Like most old forms of taxation, it was only paid by the more prosperous members of the community. Up to 1782 the returns list occupants and tax due; thereafter, owners as well as occupants are identified. The assessments, incidentally, are unreliable as guides to the contemporary value of the property as, like rateable values today, they were usually long out of date. Most of these returns are in the CROs, though some are in the PRO at Kew.

Rather more useful, perhaps, are the Hearth Tax returns for the period between 1662 and 1689. The precursor of the Land Tax, the Hearth Tax levied a charge of 2 shillings (10p) on every hearth. It was payable by the occupier rather than the owner, though some people, with a house in town and another (or others) in the country, appear more than once in the returns. People with goods worth less than £10 or occupying houses valued at less than £1 a year were exempt. Although these figures seem very low, it meant that, according to Christopher Hill, 'at least one-third of the households of England were exempt from the Hearth Tax on grounds of poverty.' (The Century of Revolution, 1961). Besides the occupants of these, there were paupers and others who had no hearth and therefore paid no tax. Nevertheless, the returns include a large number of people; if your late 17th-century ancestors were reasonably prosperous, there is a good chance of finding them in the Hearth Tax returns, which have survived in fairly good condition. The returns for 1664 also list some non-payers of the tax and are therefore especially helpful. Since they list the number of hearths in each house, the returns offer a rough guide to the relative prosperity of the taxpayers. They also help in locating addresses more precisely (you will, of course, need to know where your ancestors lived in order to locate them among the returns), and reveal the names of immediate neighbours.

In its often desperate search for revenue to match expenditure, the government resorted to all manner of strange taxes at various times, and records of these may be found either at the PRO or at the CROs. The bricked-up windows still to be seen in many Georgian houses are witnesses of the Window Tax, a similar expedient to the Hearth Tax, in which the tax payable was rated by the number of windows in the house. Some people preferred to live in gloom in order to achieve a lower rating. This unpopular tax lasted from 1696 to 1851. At different times in the 18th century, taxes were levied on carriages, servants, game, hair-powder for wigs, and a number of other surprising things. The returns are not all available, but if you hope to obtain further clues frm these sources, you should start your inquiries at the local CRO.

The CROs also held the poll books, compiled after parliamentary elections in the 18th century, which list those entitled to vote. These were the famous 40-shilling freeholders; those who owned property of lesser or no value were not entitled to vote. The poll books were published for each county and are organised by hundred (a mediaeval land system) and parish; usefully, they give the addresses of those who were entitled to vote locally but had their residence elsewhere. The Great Reform Act of 1832 broadened the franchise, and since then electoral rolls of each parish have been kept. A few of them have been printed; others are retained by the parish or are deposited in the CRO. Universal adult suffrage is of course a comparatively modern phenomenon. It was not introduced by the 1832 act nor by the acts of 1867 or 1884. Women did not gain the right to vote until 1918 (if over thirty) or 1928 (over 21).

An extract from the assessments for the 17th-century Hearth Tax, including (usefully) the names of people in the parish who were not required to pay. E 179/160.

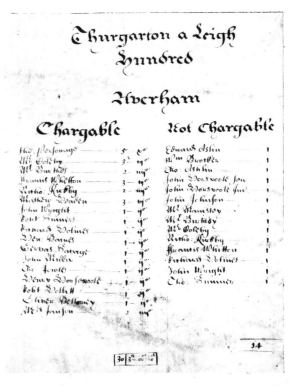

Some Other Sources

On the whole, the more successful in life your ancestors were, the easier it is to trace them. On the other hand, if they were notably unsuccessful in one way or another, they may be more easily traced than if they were just comfortable ordinary people. As previously mentioned, there is often a better chance of finding some account of paupers among parish records than more fortunate people.

Bankruptcy is a misfortune which can overtake anyone and, as readers of Dickens know, debt could land you in prison, usually the Fleet. The registers of the Fleet Prison are now in the PRO; they cover the period from 1685 to 1842. Bankrupcies were reported in the press, such as the *London Gazette* (from the 17th century) and in the depressingly titled *Perry's Bankrupt and Insolvent Gazette*. Records of the Court of Bankrupty are in the PRO and are indexed by name.

There is nothing like committing a sensational murder to get your name in the papers; should you have an ancestor with a criminal record, you may discover more about him than if he had been an average, law-abiding citizen. In the past, criminal offences were in general more numerous than they are now; not all crimes of the past seem heinous today. You are likely to feel some indignation at discovering an ancestor who was hanged for stealing the proverbial sheep.

For most of the 19th century there are annual criminal registers in the PRO, arranged by county. The records of the Assize Courts, which tried serious offences, are also in the PRO, and the Minute Books for some counties go back to Tudor times. Unfortunately, it is not easy to locate an individual case in the Minute Books, but once you have found it, you will be able to lay your hands comparatively quickly on the relevant Indictment, which gives more detail of the case.

Lesser offences were dealt with by the Quarter Sessions, presided over by the local magistrates or J.P.s (justices of the peace), and records are normally at the CRO. The Quarter Sessions were also concerned with administrative matters, such as granting licences to shopkeepers. Their records are voluminous, and possibly for that reason they have not been used as much as might be expected.

Crimes of a sensational nature, especially involving eminent people, were reported at length in the newspapers; press accounts of a trial often give more details (not always correct) of the case. Once you have located a trial through the registers, Minute Books of the Assize Courts, or the Quarter Sessions rolls, it is always worth checking local newspapers of the appropriate date.

There is almost no end to the variety of documentary records which may throw some light on the lives of your ancestors. Since no two family histories are the same and the task of researching them is different in every case, it would be pointless, boring and no doubt impossible to attempt to make a comprehensive list of all the sources that could be of use. Apart from the main repositories described in earlier chapters, there is no single indispensable source of information, but a great number of possible ones. And, once you have exhausted the obvious sources – private information, birth, marriage and death certificates, Census returns and wills – you will no doubt already have become an experienced enough genealogist to continue your research in the directions indicated by your knowledge so far.

However, there are certain promising areas which may offer vital facts in a large enough number of cases to make them worth mentioning here. Moreover, some of them tend to be overlooked even by professional researchers.

One of the more obvious of these areas is education. Something has already been said of the universities, and the usefulness of their registers for certain professions in particular. Schools may also have registers of former pupils. Of course, until the Elementary Education Act of 1870, a great number of children had little or no formal schooling, while the children of the rich were often educated privately. However, since the 16th century a great many children were educated not only at the so-called public schools (they ought properly to be called 'private' schools), but also at the grammar schools, many of which came into existence after the Reformation to replace the lost monastic schools. (The typical public school, incidentally, is not an ancient establishment like Winchester or Eton but a red-brick Victorian foundation.) There are published histories of several of the public schools and old grammar schools, which you will obviously wish to read if you know your ancestor attended (or taught at) one of them. They are naturally unlikely to tell you whether he did or not, unless he gained a prominent position in later life or became a benefactor of the school. Many schools kept registers which have been published, and possibly a greater number still possess registers which have not. They often give not only the parents of the pupil but also outline his subsequent career. The school may well possess other documents of equal relevance, so you should contact the headmaster or headmistress to inquire. You may even find that someone associated with the school is currently engaged in preparing a history of it. In the case of schools that no longer exist, there may be registers or other records at the CRO.

In the course of amassing private information from family sources, you may come across old documents of various kinds which suggest further lines of inquiry. Educational certificates or diplomas are one example; you may also find a record of membership in some learned society, a menu for a society dinner, bank statements, an insurance policy, bills, receipts, etc.

Bank statements are of course confidential, but banks may be prepared to reveal information relating to customers long dead. Very likely, the bank concerned no longer exists; early banking practice was not very strictly controlled and a number of banks, especially those which issued their own banknotes, failed. However, comparatively few banks just disappear; they are more often taken over by a larger enterprise, and the records of one of the numerous private banks of the 18th or 19th centuries may still be held by its contemporary successor. They reveal names and addresses as well as the financial prosperity of their customers; you may also find other interesting information concerning sale or purchase of property, etc.

The chances of finding old insurance company records are slighter, largely because insurance companies tend to discard obsolete files and registers. However, if you are lucky enough to locate an old insurance proposal form, it may provide you with a great many details not easily found elsewhere. Nowadays, insurance ocmpanies usually require a medical examination before they insure a life, but in days when medical examinations were less reliable, they often based the risk on other factors – the circumstances of the insured and of his relatives. Thus you may find listed the names, ages or death dates of all the members of the insured person's immediate family. The information will have to be checked against birth or death certificates, since it is not always reliable: the desire to create an impression of good health and longevity in the family may have given rise to some tinkering with the statistics.

Besides the family bible and, of course, old diaries or scrapbooks if you are lucky enough to find any, another possible source of private information, not only culinary, is Grandmama's cookbook. The genealogist Gerald Hamilton-Edwards found one in his own family which was compiled in the early 19th century and contained recipes for such items as 'Mrs Tyeth's plain cake', 'An Excellent Pudding in accordance with Mrs Lloyd's receipt', 'Mrs Thomas of Dickett's receipt for furniture paste' and 'Mrs Coster's plain Cake'. Mrs Coster was his great-grandmother, Mrs Tyeth his great-great-grandmother, Mrs Lloyd his great-great-aunt, and Mrs Thomas a friend of the family. Whatever the worth of the pudding, the cakes and the furniture paste, the old cook book was certainly a rich store of genealogical information.

If other books have survived in the family for two or more generations, they are certainly worth inspecting. Apart from the intrinsic interest of the titles, which may cast light on your forbears' tastes and interests, they may contain inscriptions or notes. It is surprising how often, even in non-literary households, one comes across autographed and inscribed copies of books by well-known authors, letters or newspaper cuttings inserted between the pages, marginal notes by the book's original owner, etc. In Victorian times people were more inclined to write notes in the margins of books, or to underline passages they wished to remember, than we are today; deplorable though the habit may be, it can be a rewarding one for their descendants. Whenever you come across books that have been in the family for a long time, it is worth flipping through the pages on the off-chance of finding a revealing note, a page from a letter of other document – or even a curl of your great-grandmother's hair!

Names

Surnames

Surnames are the basic clues of the genealogist. They are the keys which will, with luck, unlock the hidden genealogy, and they can also advance your research in many incidental ways. They may also conceal many a snare and encourage many a delusion.

Any number of interesting family connections have turned up in the past through a procedure as simple as looking up names in a telephone directory. Most large libraries in the United Kingdom have a complete set of telephone directories nowadays, and so do some large libraries overseas, such as the New York Public Library. If you want to consult the directory for one particular area, and you do not have easy access to a copy, it is always possible to obtain one through the British Post Office Telecommunications Headquarters. It is not necessary to go to Birmingham to find out if anyone with your name lives there! On the other hand, this line of inquiry is less promising if your family name, or surname, is a very common one: you have only to look up the number of Smiths in the London directory to see why (there are approximately 2,000 of them). For the overseas visitor with few clues as to the geographical origins of the ancestors he or she is looking for, it is very desirable to have an uncommon surname. Very often, however, the inquirer will know (or believe he knows) the place of origin, and in that case even a relatively common name may turn up in only moderate numbers in the local telephone directory.

It is surprising how uneven the distribution of many of the less common surnames is, and this can often give a clue to the place of origin of a family. If you find a large number of people of your name in a particular district, you may well suspect that this is the area your ancestors came from. This is not necessarily so, however; possibly the name originated elsewhere and one branch of the family who happened to move to the district you have located proved very productive of sons, while those who remained in the original home produced mainly daughters. You must bear in mind too that the number you come across is probably relevant only in relation to total population and to past population movements. Twenty examples in London, for example, are less significant than two or three in a small provincial town.

When you have found people sharing your surname in the town or district where you believe your family originated, the next step is to circularise all the individuals concerned, explaining your purpose, describing everything you know of the particular ancestor or ancestors you are trying to trace, if there are any, and any other information which may suggest that your correspondents are related to you. This may sound like a hit-or-miss form of research, as indeed it is, and it will surely result in a large number of negative or non-replies but it is a good way to start if you have nothing better to go on. If you have some idea of a particular ancestor (or ancestors) living in a particular town or district, it may lead to surprising results.

Surnames can themselves offer hints about origins, although it would be unwise to place much faith in this approach. The fact that your name is Butcher may indeed mean that one of your ancestors was a butcher, but even if true, it was too long ago to be useful. Many English surnames did originate as descriptions of a man's trade (Carpenter, Smith, Miller, Wright, etc.) but many that seem to have done so did not. Names like Bishop and Abbot do not imply an ecclesiastical ancestry, nor does King derive from royal blood. The original possessors of those names were possibly servants of the officials concerned, or played the relevant parts in a pageant.

Perhaps the commonest type of surname derived

from a man's place of residence (Hill, Brook, Bridges, Underdown, etc.). Such names sometimes refer to something as local as a tree (Oakes) or something as large as a country (Fleming), and originally most of them would have been preceded by prepositions (sometimes retained, as in Under-down). There is no truth in the notion that a 'de' or a 'le' in front of a name implies ownership of land, though it sometimes did, nor in the common belief that the dropping of the preposition marks the point in time when the name ceased to be merely an informal description and became an in-herited surname.

This manner of acquiring surnames can lead to confusion when two or more families are found in the same village with the same name. It is natural to assume that they are related, especially if the name is an uncommon one, but the true reason for the coincidence may be that several different people were named after a particular feature of the local landscape.

Many surnames derive from actual places, which you can check in a gazetteer, but at this late stage it is on the whole improbable that finding the topo-graphical source, however interesting in itself, will be of any help in tracing your forbears. Some ex-amples of surnames derived from places in the county of Norfolk are Blakeney, Calthorpe, Eccles, Filby, Harling, Heydon, Needham, Ormesby, Pal-grave and Walsingham. If you are a Heydon, there is a chance that you are related to the eponymous squirearchical family of that attractive village, and you will probably be able either to confirm or deny the supposition, since the parish registers of Hey-don are almost complete from 1538. But if you are a Blakeney, for example, you are less likely to find any evidence to connect you with that once-thriv-ing port; indeed your name may have derived from Mount Blakeney in Co. Limerick, home of the popular 18th-century general, Lord Blakeney, who commanded the defence of Minorca when Admiral Byng failed to relieve it (with fatal results to him-self) in 1756.

Many surnames have been shown to have de-scended from two or more independent sources. Thus, an Emmet or Emmot may derive from a place in Lancashire or from the woman's name Emma. The ancestor of a Gale may have been a merry fellow or he may have had some connection with a prison (gaol).

Certain surnames are of course associated with particular districts, though not derived from them. This is particularly notable in places such as the fishing villages of north-east Scotland, where there were so many people of the same surname that they were often identified by added nicknames. There were 29 George Cowies in Buckie in the mid 19th century, 68 Watts in Gardenstown (population about 1200) and 84 Mairs in wee Portknockie. At the end of the 18th century a large proportion of the thriving town of Haddington, near Edinburgh, were called Begbie, Carfrae, Dudgeon, Hepburn, Lowdan, Sheriff or Skirvane, mostly names rather uncommon elsewhere.

Nicknames sometimes became surnames (Little, Blackie, Armstrong) though probably less than is often believed. There is a tendency to assume that surnames are derived from nicknames when no other etymology appears obvious; however, even if a surname was derived from a nickname, the actual nickname may not have been the superfi-cially obvious one. The name Low, for example, probably did not refer to short stature, nor to coarse behaviour (nor to a residence at the bottom of the valley), but derived from the French term for wolf. This is just one example of the way sur-names, to someone not expert in the subject, can be more misleading than helpful. The original Mr Deadman was not revived from the dead; the name is simply a corrupt form of Debenham.

Names ending in 's', 'son' and 'ing' indicate a family relationship. Richards or Richardson were originally 'Richard's son', while the Anglo-Saxon suffix 'ing' denoted a member of a tribal group or clan. In Scotland and Ireland the prefixes 'Mac' and 'O' originally meant 'son of', as did the Welsh 'ap', and there are a number of other less common forms meaning the same thing. They originated before the use of surnames became common, which happened more recently than many people realise. Although some surnames existed in Anglo-Saxon England, they were not in common use among the population at large until the late Middle Ages (sooner in counties near London, later in the more remote provinces). This is of course long enough ago to cover most genealogical research; in fact too long ago for most people to be able to trace the original possessor of their family name. If you do reach the stage of attempting to track down me-diaeval forbears, the absence of a hereditary sur-name can complicate matters considerably.

The earliest surnames usually belonged to pow-erful landowners who were called after their es-tates. However, it does not follow that someone possessing such a surname today is descended from an early mediaeval nobleman; tenants and servants often adopted their lord's name. Not all Howards are related to the present duke of Norfolk, nor all Churchills to the duke of Marlborough.

Surnames were more widely adopted, partly at least, because Christian names like John or Thomas were becoming so common that it was difficult to identify individuals by their first name only. An interesting example of how a patronymic – a sur-name taken from a father's first name – was adopted can be found in the Scottish Exechequer

Rolls. An entry in 1428 refers to one 'Jacobus filius Johannis de Hollandia . . .' The following year the name appears in English: 'James, son of John of Holland . . .'. By 1431 it is 'James Johnson of Holland', and in the final version simply 'Jacobus Johnsoun' (James Johnson). Patronymics were not at first permanent surnames: the son of James Johnson would probably have had the surname 'Jamesson' rather than Johnson. In remote parts of Scotland this custom continued until surprisingly recent times – well into the 19th century in Shetland, where one finds a long line of alternative generations named Magnus Johnson and John Magnusson.

Surnames were quite often changed for one reason or another in the Middle Ages and in later times. William Tyndale was known in Gloucestershire as Huchyns, while Oliver Cromwell's forbears were named Williams (one of them changed the name in honour of his uncle, Thomas Cromwell, a minister of Henry VIII). There is a fairly typical reference in a 15th-century document to one 'Nichol Wigh otherwise called Nicholas Ketringham otherwise called John Segrave otherwise called Nicholl 'Pecche'. Surnames were often applied in the first instance by someone else, perhaps a clerk making out a legal document, not by the person to whom they were applied. A man might take the name of a person or relative who left him property; occasionally a man would take his wife's name, rather than vice-versa, because her social status was superior to his. Hyphenated names often arose in this way. Servants sometimes took their masters' names, slaves often did, and so did apprentices, though usually only during their apprenticeship. Foundlings (deserted infants) were often given the name of the local ward or church. Over 100 foundlings baptised in the Temple in London between 1728 and 1755 were given the name Temple or Templar.

Sometimes people changed their names simply because they did not like the one they were born with – it requires a certain moral stamina to go through life with the name Bogg or Smellie – or because they wished to conceal their origins. Many Jewish names were anglicised whilst other immigrants from Eastern Europe and Scandinavia often found it advisable to adopt a form of their name more easily pronounced in English, or less obviously foreign. Edward Lear's Danish grandfather was called Lør. If you suspect a name change, it can be difficult to track down, since British subjects (but not aliens) are free to change their names without any formal declaration. For the sake of

Deed poll which shows the prediliction of European immigrants, especially from the east, for anglicising their 'unpronounceable' names.

R O C K W E L L) BY THIS DEED (which is intended to be enrolled in the Enrolment Department
(RACHWALSKY)) of the Central Office of the Royal Courts of Justice) I the undersigned ERWIN
) LUDWIG ROCKWELL of 36 Barn Rise Wembley Park Middlesex and now or lately
a) called Erwin Ludwig Rachwalsky a naturalized British subject do hereby for
) myself my wife and my children and remoter issue absolutely renounce relinquish
DEED POLL) and abandon the use of my said surname of Rachwalsky and assume adopt and
10/- 2978) determine to take and use from the date hereof the surname of ROCKWELL in
substitution of my former surname of Rachwalsky, AND in pursuance of such
change of surname as aforesaid I HEREBY DECLARE that I shall at all times hereafter in all
records deeds documents and other writings and in all actions and proceedings as well as in
all dealings and transactions and upon all occasions whatsoever use and subscribe the said
name of ROCKWELL as my surname in substitution for my former surname of Rachwalsky so - - -
renounced as aforesaid to the intent that I my wife and my children and issue may hereafter
be called known or distinguished not by the former surname of Rachwalsky but by the surname
of ROCKWELL only.- -
AND I HEREBY AUTHORISE and request all persons at all times to designate describe and- - -
address myself my wife and my children and remoter issue by the adopted surname of ROCKWELL
only- -
IN WITNESS whereof I have hereunto subscribed my Christian names of Erwin Ludwig and my
assumed surname of ROCKWELL and also my said former surname of Rachwalsky this twentieth day of
November, 1946 and have affixed my seal -

SIGNED SEALED AND DELIVERED)
by the above-named Erwin)   ERWIN LUDWIG ROCKWELL
Ludwig Rachwalsky and)   (L.S.)
Erwin Ludwig Rockwell)   (ERWIN LUDWIG RACHWALSKY)
in the presence of : -)

Ernest Martin Foulkes
 54 Barn Rise
 Wembley Hill, Middx.
 Managing Director

Kathleen A. Jeans
 74 Harefield Rd,
 Uxbridge, M'sex.

Declaration filed & Certificate of Naturalization No AZ 20415 produced A.H.P.- - - - - - -

ENROLLED in the Central Office of the Supreme
Court of Judicature the Twentysecond day of
November in the year of Our Lord 1946

convenience, fortunately, they usually do adopt some formal procedure, of which the most likely is by deed poll. A record of these is kept at the PRO, mostly indexed by name. If you know either the original name or the new one, the change can usually be traced.

Spelling was not standardised until the 18th century and indeed, as far as names go, it is not completely standardised even now. The example of Shakespeare is often quoted to show how many different versions of one man's name can be found, and even a more simple name, like Coxon or Dyke, may appear in half a dozen variations. When checking old records for a particular name, therefore, you must be alert to variant spellings. One amateur genealogist was searching a parish register for the baptism of a baby with the surname Darren and eventually found it under 'T', spelled 'Terrin'! People tended to write names as they were pronounced, and the local dialect can therefore be expected to show an effect on spelling. It is important, when copying names from old documents, to make sure you copy exactly the spelling used there. Puzzling variants are common enough without introducing new ones. Many genealogists develop a sixth sense about names and their likely variants, but that is something that comes only with experience.

The origin of surnames and their topography are fascinating subjects in themselves, although not necessarily helpful in tracing ancestors. If you are called Dodd, Duckett, Dunning or Darwin, you may well have had Anglo-Saxon ancestors. If Dring or Drummond, you may derive from some Viking settler, but in no case, of course, is there any hope of tracing the man responsible. Similarly, it is true that surnames ending in 'son' tend to be more common in the north of England than in the south, probably as a result of Scandinavian influence. However, it goes without saying that you cannot suppose your family came from the north just because your name is Robinson or Jobson.

The same, unfortunately, is true of alleged Celtic origins. In Wales, hereditary surnames date only from about the 16th century or later. Before that Welshmen were described as, for instance, John ap Madoc ap Gryffyd. Genealogically, such names can be very helpful, and indeed the adoption of fixed, inherited surnames is not always a blessing. Wales is a good example of a country where surnames are relatively few in number; the large quantity of Joneses and Williamses can make the genealogist's task confusing. In Islam, where the patronymic system has not yet taken over, a man's full name will tell you not only his own personal name, but the personal name of his eldest son, of his father, grandfather and perhaps great-grandfather, and the place he comes from – unwieldy but informative.

In the Highlands of Scotland this custom continued into the early 18th century, when one comes across names like Malcolm MacIain mhic Mhurchaidh (Malcolm son of John son of Murdoch).

Such typically Welsh names as Jones, Williams or Edwards, while they may strongly suggest Welsh origins, do not prove them. In Scotland, surnames originated a little earlier than in Wales, but they were still quite rare in the 15th century. They were a particularly late development in the Highlands, where, as a result of the clan system, the same surname was often shared by a large group. People with typically Highland surnames usually assume that they are members of the clan indicated, but this may be true only in a very loose sense, if at all. Originally, the clan name was borne only by the chief and his immediate family. Other members of the clan, when they came to adopt hereditary surnames, often took the clan name. The clans were less exclusive than is often thought, and smaller groups, perhaps seeking protection from a powerful clan chief nearby, would adopt the clan name although they were unrelated. Those who accepted the protection of Gilbert Cumin, lord of Glenchearnach, received a rough kind of clan baptism in the hens' trough near the door of the castle; they were subsequently known as 'Cumins of the hen trough' (*Cuminich clach nan cearc*) to distinguish them from the true Cumins. A friend of Sir Walter Scott on a shooting holiday in Scotland encountered a keeper named Gordon whom he thought he recognised as the same man who had guided him on a previous occasion, but then known as Macpherson. On being asked if this was so, the man replied that it was, 'but that was when I lived on the other side of the hill'. There are probably people named Macdonald today who, far from being as they suppose members of Clan Donald, are descended from someone called Donald Campbell, and are thus members by blood of the Macdonalds' arch enemies. Additional complications were introduced in comparatively recent times by the Irish immigrants who entered south-west Scotland in considerable numbers. According to the author of *Galloway Gossip*, in the early 19th century, 'Twa men frae Ireland cam ower to make drains for Col. Andrew McDouall of Logan, for he was a horrid man for improvements, and had hundreds of Irish frainin till him. Yin o' the twa they ca't O'Toole, an' the ither O'Dowd, and they both married and settled in the Rhinns an' their sons became Mr. Doyle and Mr. Doud. The grandchildren now call themselves McDouall and Dodds.' Many other races of course contributed, in Scotland as well as England and Wales. 'The Scots (originally Irish, but by now Scotch) were at this time inhabiting Ireland, having driven the Irish (Picts) out of Scotland; while the Picts

55

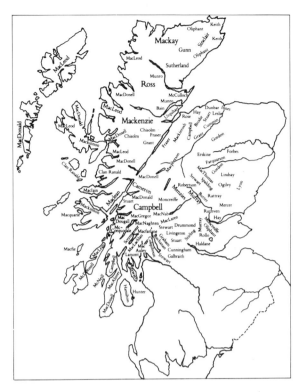

Clan map of the Highlands and Brae Country of Scotland in the 16th-century, illustrating the spheres of influence of the clans and their families.

Lindsay and Hamilton are English, Lamont and MacLeod from Scandinavia. If, incidentally, you are a Pole named Machlejd, you undoubtedly had a MacLeod ancestor. Although clan names still predominate in their original areas of residence, the splitting off of small groups, often caused by a growing population, has made the clan map a great deal more complicated than it looks in most of the versions one sees printed today.

Just as possession of a clan name does not mean that you are necessarily a member of that clan by blood, Celtic surnames in general do not necessarily imply Celtic descent, just as Anglo-Saxon surnames do not necessarily imply *non*-Celtic descent. A man takes his name from his father only, but his lineage is equally divided between his father and his mother. In short, surnames are seldom an entirely reliable guide to race or place. You could conceivably be a non-Cornish Trevelyan, a non-Welsh Jones or a non-Scottish Fraser, and although it is highly probable that the original possessors of the names *were* respectively Cornish, Welsh and Scottish, they lived far too long ago to be traced and may represent an insignificant proportion of your ancestry. As topographical guides, surnames may well offer important clues, but they are also likely to be either misleading or irrelevant.

(originally Scots) were now Irish (living in brackets) and *vice versa*. It is essential to keep these distinctions clearly in mind . . .' (*1066 and All That*). Quite!

The history of the clans, though the subject of much enthusiastic research, is extremely complex and badly documented. For example, when the clan MacGregor was temporarily outlawed in the 17th century, its members adopted names like Doyle, Johnstone or Menzies. This would appear to suggest that if you are a MacGregor there is a strong presumption that you belong to the clan, since only clan members were likely to preserve the name when it was outlawed; but MacGregor is a comparatively common name today, which throws some doubt on the supposition. Somewhat later, when there was more mingling between people of the Highlands and Lowlands, Gaelic names were translated into English, not always in an easily recognisable form. Macleans became Johnsons, McLeays or McLevys became Livingstones, etc. There are many other sources of historical confusion. The clan names themselves have different origins: most of the 'Mac—s' are Gaelic and imply descent from a common ancestor, but Graham and Sutherland are topographical in origin, Anderson and Grant are of French derivation,

Christian Names

First names, or Christian names, may also be useful hints in genealogical research. As with surnames, much depends on the actual name. John, Thomas or William are, as a rule, less suggestive than Isaac or Aloysius. A Biblical name may be Jewish, or it may suggest a Puritan origin. Old Testament names are still popular among members of certain strict Protestant sects, though one seldom comes across that curious Puritan affection for adopting whole verses of the Psalms; as in the case of the Puritan parents who named their unfortunate son, 'Bind-their-kings-in-chains-and-their-nobles-in-links-of-iron'. Foreign names naturally suggest foreign origin, a French name in the early 18th century, for example, suggesting Huguenot connections. James and Charles in the same period may indicate Jacobite sympathies – you certainly would not expect to come across the name George in a Jacobite family. Children were sometimes named after famous contemporary people or events. According to the Birth Announcements in *The Times*, at least one child was named Jubilee to commemorate Queen Elizabeth II's twenty-five years on the throne. Of babies born in Tottenham in 1938, according to the registrar, no less than twenty per cent bore names of currently popular film stars. In 1981 the name Diana showed a rise in popularity as a result, no doubt, of the engagement and marriage of the Prince of Wales to Lady Diana Spencer. Unusual first names are often a guide to date. Should you come across a relative named after one of the duke of Wellington's victories in the Napoleonic wars, you can make a fairly safe guess at the year of his birth.

In Britain, unlike some other countries, parents can give their children any name they wish. However, the general tendency, especially among the middle and upper classes, has always been conservative, especially in certain periods. The chiefs of Clan Campbell, for example, were called Archibald, Colin or John (with a couple of Duncans thrown in) for twenty generations, from the 14th to the 19th century. The custom in Scotland was generally to name the eldest son after his father's father, the second son after his mother's father, and the third after his father. Daughters were often named similarly, the first after her mother's mother, the second after her father's mother, the third after her mother. This custom sometimes becomes useful when figuring out family relationships and relative ages of children. In England, too, the eldest son was often named after his father or grandfather; if you find among a long line of Johns and Alfreds an exceptional Sebastian or Philip, you will naturally view him with some suspicion. Maybe his parents suddenly rebelled against family tradition, or wished to humour a rich and unmarried relative, but maybe he was not a relative at all and has crept into the family tree through error.

The fashion for using surnames as first names began in the 16th century – Winston was a fairly early example in the Churchill family – and in some families has proved useful in tracking down marriages or collateral branches of the family; the name in question is almost invariably the surname of some relative or the mother's maiden name. At that time few people had more than one Christian name. The custom of having two or more did not begin until the 17th century, the royal family giving the lead in this as in many other conventions, although it was not until the end of the next century did this become common. The 18th-century writer Oliver Goldsmith named a character Carolina Wilhelmina Amelia Skeggs to poke fun at the current fashion for giving girls a string of romantic names, despite the earthiness of their surnames.

Christian names, like hairstyles or clothes, are subject to fashion. In the late Tudor period names drawn from classical history and mythology became popular. In the 18th century there was a vogue for old English names. Sometimes hitherto unknown names are adopted by some well-known family and rapidly became popular. The girl's name Karen is now quite common in England; but, a generation or two ago, if you met a woman named Karen you would probably have assumed her family was of foreign origin. This example, and a number of others, can probably be ascribed to American influence: the mix of nationalities in the United States has resulted in many first names derived from non-British traditions gaining popularity.

Names also appear to move up and down the social scale in an intriguing way. Recently, Sarah was especially popular among well-to-do and 'county' families, but a couple of generations earlier it was, typically, a working-class name: in a popular play of the times, the maid, not the mistress, would be called Sarah.

Trade Names

Certain legal documents give a man's, or woman's, trade or profession as an additional aid to identification (which in former times, as we have seen, was often the way in which many surnames were first acquired). Obviously this can be invaluable in establishing as full a history of your family as possible, not just a family tree to connect you with a particular ancestor.

Great caution must be exercised when identifying a trade because, for a number of reasons, the description may not mean quite what it seems to mean. People did not always describe their occupations accurately or honestly; the names of certain trades have changed their meaning whilst some people had more than one trade. A classic case of how confusion can arise even among scholars is that of Izaak Walton, the 17th-century writer best known for his book on fishing, *The Compleat Angler*. A good deal has always been known of Walton's life, but, curiously enough, very little about his professional occupation. His 18th-century biographers described him as a linen draper, but there was no known documentary evidence of this, and in the mid-19th century, as a result of new discoveries, it was established that he was an ironmonger. What seemed to be clinching evidence was that he was described as an ironmonger on his marriage certificate and that he was, without doubt, a long-serving member of the London Ironmongers' Company (one of the City livery companies or guilds). However, membership of a City livery company does not mean, now or then, that the man concerned actually practised that trade. King Edward III was a member of the guild of linen-armourers, although we may legitimately doubt if he knew one end of a needle from the other. Nevertheless, in every book which referred to him from the mid-19th century almost to the present, Izaak Walton was described as an ironmonger by trade. Recent research in the PRO turned up new documents in which he was identified as in one case a sempster (tailor) and in another as a draper. In other words, the old 18th-century authorities were perfectly correct, and the evidence that suggested Walton was an ironmonger amounted to a great red herring.

People were sometimes tempted to 'improve' their social status by giving their occupation a grander name than it deserved. An agricultural labourer who kept a couple of pigs and grew a few turnips in his garden might be tempted to call himself a farmer. But even when there was no intent to deceive, confusion can easily arise. Most people are aware that clergymen were often called 'clerks' in former times, but other changes in terminology are not so obvious. The trade of 'fisherman', for example, would suggest to most of us a maritime existence, but up to the late 19th century there were plenty of men making a living on rivers and lakes far from the sea who might have described themselves as fishermen. Thomas Milbourne, who died about 1880, was one of these. He lived at Hampton in Middlesex and provided boats, bait and advice to anglers from London. But he is elsewhere described as a coal merchant, while another member of his family was alternatively 'fisherman' and 'grocer'.

Other Names

In our egalitarian age, forms of address are slowly going out of fashion. Few people would now know the correct, formal way to address the wife of an earl, for example, and the old form 'Esquire' after a gentleman's name is used only as a courtesy, if at all. But in earlier times forms of address had a more precise meaning and, when they appear in old documents, they should not be ignored, because they tell something about the social status of the person concerned. The social hierarchy in England, though always more open to change than is generally believed, was nevertheless much more rigid than it is today. Even the clothes people wore, or the carriages they drove, were a reflection of their position in society.

Besides names and titles of people, you will probably have to deal with topographical names. These too have often altered over the centuries; reorganizations of local government have resulted in, for example, some villages appearing to migrate unpredictably from one country to the next. It is not, as a rule, difficult to locate places whose names have changed. Thomas Barker, another fisherman and approximate contemporary of Izaak Walton, declared in print that he was born at Bracemeal in Shropshire, and that fact has been repeated by everyone who has had occasion to mention Thomas Barker since. None of these modern writers, apparently, troubled to look at a map or a gazetteer as, if they had done so, they would have found that no such place as Bracemeal exists. But it is a simple matter to find out where it was. The famous atlas of John Speed, compiled in the early 17th century, shows a place called Bracemeal near Shrewsbury, and comparison with a modern map shows that it is now called Meole Brace.

Not all such topographical problems, it must be said, are solved quite so easily, but one has to go a long way back in history to find place names which can no longer be identified. The Institute of Heraldic and Genealogical Studies in Canterbury publishes a number of maps of special interest to genealogists, and if your ancestors came from a particular county in England or Wales it will be worthwhile obtaining a copy of the appropriate genealogical map. Various editions of Ordnance Survey maps can be consulted in the larger libraries or obtained through Her Majesty's Stationery Office. The largest scale of the Ordnance Survey maps shows every lamp-post, practically every brick, but the 6 inch:1 mile maps, which show individual buildings, are large enough for most purposes.

Heraldry

Heraldry, the study of armorial bearings, is a different subject from genealogy and will probably not concern the majority of people who are engaged in a hunt for their ancestors. However, quite a large number of people do have the right to a coat of arms. Some families undoubtedly have that right without knowing it, while other families boast a coat of arms to which they have no right whatever. Some people's interest in tracing their ancestors is sparked off in the first place by a belief that they are entitled to bear arms.

Heraldry is a curious and complicated subject with an intriguingly arcane terminology of its own. However, there is not space in this book to provide more than the briefest outline of its nature.

Originally, only kings and nobles bore arms, but as time went on the right was extended more widely, eventually encompassing corporations, commercial institutions, etc., as well as individuals. Like many picturesque conventions, the original purpose was a thoroughly practical one. It was essentially a means of identification. Leaders in war seem to have worn a badge or device, like the Roman eagle, in ancient times, but modern heraldry dates from the Middle Ages, and probably developed, partly at least, from the use of personal seals on documents. Arms displayed on shields did not become widespread until the 13th century. In a battle, it was impossible to tell who was who without some easily spotted identification, and the armed men of each knight usually wore a simple design or geometric device. At first, it had no special significance but soon became in some way personalized. Many of the early designs were based on a visual pun, like trumpets for Trumpington, salamanders for Salle, pike (luce) for Lucy, or mallets for Malet. Later, less obvious symbols were adopted, usually relating to a notable incident in the bearer's history or character. The lion was popular because of its reputation as a beast of cour-

age. Mediaeval knights wearing full armour with helmet could not be identified even face to face: William the Conqueror had to remove his helmet at the Battle of Hastings to convince his men that he was still alive. But distinctively decorated shields, standards and surcoats overcame this problem. 'You know me by my habit', as the French herald remarks to Shakespeare's Henry V. Shakespeare also reminds us that the system could be perverted to cause confusion among the enemy: the Earl of Douglas, battling for the rebellious Percies in *Henry IV Part I*, slaughters one royal decoy after another, complaining, 'Another king! they grow like Hydra's heads.'

Coats of arms, which soon became hereditary, were a symbol of family pride and of the status of the bearer in feudal society. The rather puzzling term 'coat' probably derives from the fact that the arms were often displayed on the linen surcoat (as well as on shield, banner and almost everywhere else there was room for them). The heralds, originally the king's messengers and therefore institutionally older than heraldry itself, became the officials who recorded and eventually controlled heraldic devices. Things were already getting out of hand in the time of Henry V, who issued an edict forbidding anyone to assume a coat of arms unless entitled to it by descent or through a grant by the Society of Heralds. Several types of rolls, or registers, of arms survive from the Middle Ages. From the 15th to the 17th centuries, a number of national (excluding Scotland) surveys or 'visitations' were made of those bearing arms, in which heralds visited each country and required those who bore arms to supply proof that they were entitled to do so.

A full 'achievement' of arms consists of shield, crest (surmounting the helmet), 'supporters' (such as the lion and unicorn in the Royal Arms) and, probably, a motto – frequently a recent addition enunciating some high-minded sentiment in Latin. There may also be badges, like the fleur-de-lys of the Prince of Wales, which are not connected with the shield but were often displayed on the livery of retainers as well as being liberally plastered all over the family furniture.

Today the grant of a coat of arms is governed by the Earl Marshal and the College of Arms (whose headquarters is in Victoria Street, London) on behalf of the monarch. Any armorial device not approved by the College of Arms is, strictly, illegitimate. However, the whole situation is complicated by the fact that arms, unlike a title of nobility, can descend to *all* the sons, and to all of their sons, etc. (they can also, in certain circumstances, be passed down through daughters). Therefore, if you can prove that you are a descendant in the male line from someone to whom arms were granted, you are entitled to display the coat of arms yourself. Only the eldest son, however, bore precisely the same arms as his father (after the latter's death). Younger sons bore marks of cadency (the word comes from the same root as 'cadet'), such as a cresent for the second son, a rose for the seventh son, etc, whilst a new cadency mark was added with each generation (the seventh son of a second son bearing a rose on a crescent, for example). The situation soon became impossibly complicated, and in fact cadency marks are largely disregarded today. Very few people, in any case, could work out exactly what they should be.

During the 18th century, when snobbery was probably more acute than it was in the Victorian era, many families adopted arms to which they had no right, merely to exalt their social status. In the 19th century advertisements sometimes appeared in the press promising to provide a coat of arms for anyone who sent in his surname and county of residence (one occasionally hears stories of similar operations much more recently). Many people, perhaps quite innocently, took advantage of these specious offers; there are as a result families today who believe quite wrongly that they possess a coat of arms. If you happen to have some of your great-grandmother's silver engraved with the family crest, you should be prepared to find that the crest is not genuine. On the other hand, there were plenty of armigerous ('arms-bearing') families in which, as a result of reduced social circumstances, the arms were gradually forgotten. It is, therefore, at least as probable that a man unwittingly does possess the right to arms as that the arms he so proudly displays on his printed writing paper are bogus. To find out whether the crest is genuine, you need only submit it to the College of Arms, who will identify the family to which it belongs. Should it turn out that the crest, or arms, are authentic, then of course they will prove enor-

mously helpful in your genealogical search. Incidentally, there is no law to prevent anyone adopting a coat of arms, any more than there is a law to prevent someone calling himself the Emperor of China; it is simply meaningless.

In principle, it is a fairly simple matter to discover whether you are entitled to bear arms or not. You can consult a work such as *Burke's General Armory of England, Scotland, Ireland and Wales* (1884) or *Fairbairn's Book of Crests of the Families of Great Britain and Ireland* (1968). If you find your family name, you have merely to ascertain from the College of Arms that the arms are genuine and then, rather more difficult as a rule, that they apply to your family specifically. One sometimes comes across a coat of arms assumed without authority which closely resembles the authentic arms of a more illustrious family with the same name; many hopes of a noble pedigree have been falsely aroused by such deceitful practices.

In Scotland, where these matters are more tightly organized, the chief heraldic authority is the Lyon King of Arms. The Lyon Office library is open to the public, on payment of a fee, which is not the case with the College of Arms in London (their records can normally be consulted only through one of the heralds). The loss of so many records in Ireland during the Troubles has complicated matters in this as in other genealogical areas. The Genealogical Office in Dublin is the authoritative source for Irish heraldry.

Heraldry is a subject full of pitfalls for the inexperienced, and although there are many good books about it, you will probably need expert assistance if you become involved in it. The Heraldry Society, in London, will prove helpful.

The coat of arms adopted by Christopher Columbus in 1502. Arms frequently display symbols appropriate to the activities of their bearers.

Useful Addresses

Society of Genealogists
14 Charterhouse Buildings,
Goswell Road,
London, WC1M 7BA
Telephone: 020 7251 8799

The Association of Genealogists and Researchers in Archives (AGRA)
29 Badgers Close,
Horsham, West Sussex, RH12 5RU
E-mail: agra@agra.org.uk
Web-site: www.agra.org.uk

British Record Society
Stone Barn Farm,
Sutherland Road,
Longsdon,
Staffordshire, ST9 9QD
E-mail: britishrecordsociety@hotmail.com

British Library
96 Euston Road,
London, NW1 2DB
Telephone: 020 7412 7000
Web-site: www.bl.uk

The British Museum
Great Russell Street, WC1B 3DG
Telephone: 020 7323 8605
Web-site: www.thebritishmuseum.ac.uk

The Institute of Heraldic & Genealogical Studies
Northgate,
Canterbury,
Kent, CT1 1BA
E-mail: ihgs@ihgs.ac.uk
Web-site: www.ihgs.ac.uk

Society of Australian Genealogists
Richmond Villa,
120 Kent Street,
Observatory Hill,
Sydney 2000
Australia
E-mail: info@sag.org.au

New Zealand Society of Genealogists Inc
PO Box 8795,
Symonds Street,
Auckland 1035
E-mail: nzsg-contact@genealogy.org.nz

Genealogical Society of Ireland
11 Desmond Avenue,
Dun Laoghaire, Co. Dublin,
Ireland
E-mails: GenSocIreland@iol.ie
Web-site: welcome.to/GenealogyIreland

North of Ireland Family History Society
c/o QUB School of Education,
69 University Street,
Belfast, NI BT7 1HL
E-mails: R.Sibbett@tesco.net
Web-site: www.nifhs.org

Irish Genealogical Research Society
c/o 82 Eaton Square,
London SW1W 9AJ

Useful web-sites:

Free Births, Marriages & Deaths Data
www.freebmd.rootsweb.com/cgi/search.pl

Internet Family History Association of Australia
www.shoalhaven.net.au

Civil records: Births, Marriages & Deaths
General Register Offices, Uk Libraries
www.ramsdale.org/schindex.htm

Justice Tasmania Births, Deaths & Marriages
www.justice.tas.gov.au/bdm/

Bibliography

Beginners' Guides
Beard, T. F. and Demong, D. *How to Find Your Family Roots* McGraw-Hill, 1977.
Camp, A. J. *Tracing Your Ancestors* John Gifford, 1970.
Clare, W. *Simple Guide to Irish Genealogy* Irish Genealogical Research Society, 3rd ed. 1967.
Doane, G. H. *Searching For Your Ancestors* Bantam Books, 1973.
Emmison, F. E. *Introduction to Archives* Phillimore, 1978.
Hamilton-Edwards, G. K. S. *In Search of Ancestry* Phillimore, 1976.
Hamilton-Edwards, G. K. S. *In Search of Scottish Ancestry* Phillimore, 1972.
Iredale, D. *Discovering Your Family Tree* Shire Publications, 3rd ed. 1977.
Iredale, D. *Enjoying Archives* David and Charles, 1973.
Mander, M. *How to Trace Your Ancesters* Mayflower Books, 1977.
Matthews, C. M. *Your Family History* Lutterworth Press, 1976.
Steel, D. J. *Discovering Your Family History* B.B.C., 1980.
Steel, D. J. and Taylor, L. *Family History in Schools* Phillimore, 1973.
Unett, J. *Making a Pedigree* David and Charles, 2nd ed. 1971.
Willis, A. J. *Genealogy for Beginners* Phillimore, 1979.

General Guides to Sources
Andrews, C. M. *Guide to the Material for American History to 1783, in the Public Record Office of Great Britain*, 2 vols., 1912.
British Record Association *Handlist of Scottish and Welsh Record Publications*, B.R.A. 1954.

Crick, B. R. and Alman, M. *Guide to Manuscripts Relating to America in Great Britain and Ireland* Oxford University Press, 1961.

Emmison, F. G. *Archives and Local History* Phillimore, 1974. A general survey of local history sources.

Falley, M. D. *Irish and Scotch-Irish Ancestral Research*, 1961–2.

Greenwood, V. D., *The Researcher's Guide to American Genealogy* Genealogical Publications, Chicago, 1973.

Handlin, O. and others *Harvard Guide to American History* Harvard University Press, 1954. List of publications of records, colony by colony.

Hansen, N. T. *Guide to Genealogical Sources – Australia and New Zealand*, 1963.

Her Majesty's Stationery Office *British National Archives* HMSO, 1980. List of printed records from the Public Record Office.

Her Majesty's Stationery Office *The Records of the Colonial and Dominions Offices*, HMSO, 1964. PRO Handbook No. 3.

Hoskins, W. G. *Local History in England* Longman, 1973.

Iredale, D. *Enjoying Archives* David and Charles, 1973.

Kirkham, E. K. *Research in American Genealogy* Deseret Books, 1962.

Lombard, R. J. J. *Handbook for Genealogical Research in South Africa*, 1977.

New York Public Library, *Research Libraries. Dictionary Catalog of the Local History and Genealogy Division*, N.Y.P.L. Publications, New York, 1971

Nickson, M. A. E. *The British Library: Guide to the Catalogues and Indexes of the Department of Manuscripts* Her Majesty's Stationery Office, 1975.

Pine, L. G. *Genealogist's Encyclopaedia* David and Charles, 1969.

Public Archives of Canada *Tracing Your Ancestors in Canada*, 1972.

Richardson, J. *The Local Historian's Encyclopaedia* Historical Publications, Orchard House, 54 Station Road, New Barnet, Herts, 1974.

Roberts, S. and others, *Research Libraries and Collections in the United Kingdom* Clive Bingley, 1978.

Rottenberg, D. *Finding our Fathers* Random House, New York, 1977. A Guidebook to Jewish Genealogy.

Royal Ministry for Foreign Affairs, Stockholm *Finding Your Forefathers: Some Hints for Americans of Swedish Origin*, 1976.

Rubincam, M. *Genealogical Research Methods and Sources*, Genealogical Publications, Chicago, 1966.

Rye, W. *Records and Record Searching*, Genealogical Publications, Chicago, 1969.

Sandison, A. *Tracing Ancestors in Shetland*, Shetland Times, 1978.

Smith, C. N. and A. P. C. *Encyclopaedia of German-American Genealogical Research*, Bowker, New York, 1976.

Smith, F. and Gardner, D. E. *Genealogical Research in England and Wales*, 3 vols. Salt Lake City: Bookcraft, 1956–59, 1964. A standard work with volumes on *1.* Civil registration, census returns, and parish registers; *2.* Military and naval records, plus county by county directory to available records; *3.* Handwriting guide.

Stephens, W. B. *Sources for English Local History*, Manchester University Press, hardback and paperback 1972.

West, J. *Village Records*, Macmillan, 1962. Useful book containing detailed descriptions of sources, together with facsimiles and transcripts of documents. Each section also lists, county by county, records in print.

Whyte, D. *Introducing Scottish Genealogical Research*, Scottish Genealogical Society, 1979.

The Census

Dubester, H. J. *State Censuses: An Annotated Bibliography of Population Taken after the Year 1790 by States and Territories of the Unites States*, B. Franklin, New York, 1969.

Galbraith, V. H. *An Introduction to the Use of Public Records*, Oxford University Press, 1934.

Gibson, J. S. W. *Census Returns 1841, 1851, 1861, 1871 on Microfilm: A Directory of Local Holdings*, Gulliver Press, 1979.

Guide to the Contents of the Public Record Office, 3 vols. HMSO, 1963–69. Vol. 1 *Legal Records*; Vol. 2 *State Papers and Departmental Records*; Vol. 3 *Accessions 1960–66*.

Her Majesty's Stationery Office *Abstract of Arrangements Respecting Registration of Births, Marriages and Deaths*, HMSO, 1952. Full details of all the registers kept in the United Kingdom, Commonwealth and Republic of Ireland.

Her Majesty's Stationery Office *Guide to Official Sources: Census Reports of Great Britain 1801–1931*, HMSO, 1951

Kirkham, E. K. *A Handy Guide to Census Searching in the Larger Cities of the United States*, Deseret Books, Cornville, 1974.

Kirkham, E. K. *A Survey of American Census Schedules 1790–1950*, Deseret Books, Cornville, 1961.

Parish Records (including Dissenters)

Agnew, D. C. A. *Protestant Exiles from France*, 2 vols., before and after 1681, 3rd edn., 1886.

Bloxham, V. B. and Metcalfe, D. F. *Key to Parochial Register of Scotland*, 1970

Burgess, F. B. *English Churchyard Memorials*, Lutterworth, 1963.

Burke, A. M. *Key to the Ancient Parish Registers of England and Wales*, 1908.

Evans, E. J. *Tithes and the Tithe Commutation Act 1836*, Bedford Square Press, 1978.

Freedman, M. A. *A Minority in Britain*, Vallentine, New York, 1955. Jewish history.

General Record House, Edinburgh *Detailed List of the Old Parish Registers of Scotland*, 1872.

Henshaw, W. W. *Encyclopaedia of American Quaker Genealogy*, 6 vols., 1936–50.

Humphrey-Smith, C. R. *Parish Maps of the Counties of England and Wales*, Phillimore, 1977.

Kirkham, E. K. *A Survey of American Church Records, Major Denominations before 1880*, Deseret Books, Cornville, 1971.

Local Population Studies, *Catalogue of Original Parish Registers in Record Offices and Libraries*, 1974, supplements 1976 and 1978.

Owen, D. M. *The Records of the Established Church in England*, British Records Association, 1970

Registrar General *List of Non-Parochial Registers and Records in the Custody of the Registrar General of Births, Deaths and Marriages*, 1841, 1859.

Steel, D. J. (ed.) *National Index of Parish Registers*, Phillimore: Vol. 1, *Sources for Births, Marriages and Deaths before 1837*, 1976; Vol. 2 *Sources for Nonconformist Genealogy and Family History*, 1972; Vol. 3 *Sources for Roman Catholic and Jewish Genealogy and Family History*, 1973; Vol. 12 *Sources for Scottish Genealogy and Family History*, 1971.

Stephenson, M. A. *A List of Monumental Brasses in the British Isles*, rev. edn., 1977.

Tate, W. E. *The Parish Chest*, Cambridge University Press, 1963.

Turner, G. L. *Original Records of Early Nonconformity*, 1911. Includes a list of dissenters after the Coventicle Act.

White, H. L. *Monuments and their Inscriptions*, Society of Genealogists, 1978. Practical guide to identification of styles of stone, and decipherment of inscriptions.

Research

Barnett, M. *How to Publish Genealogical and Historical Records*, 1971.

Buck, W. S. B. *Examples of Handwriting 1550–1650*, Phillimore, 1973.

Emmison, F. G. *How to Read Local Archives 1550–1700*, Phillimore, 1978.

Grieve, H. E. P. *Examples of English Handwriting 1150–1750*, rev. edn. Essex Record Office, 1966.

Hector, L. C. *The Handwriting of English Documents*, Arnold, 1966.

Johnson, C. and Jenkinson, H. *English Court Hand 1066–1500*, 1915

Martin, C. T. *The Record Interpreter*, Kohler and Coombes, 1976. Latin abbreviations and words.

Newton, K. C. *Mediaeval Local Records: A Reading Aid*, Historical Association, 1971.

Palgrave-Moore, P. T. R. *How to Record Your Family Tree*, Elvey Dowers Publications, 1979.

Pugh, R. B. *How to Write a Parish History*, Allen and Unwin, 1959.

Wills

Camp, A. J. *Wills and Their Whereabouts*, The Society of Genealogists, 1974.

Gibson, J. S. W. *Wills and Where to Find Them*, Phillimore, 1974.

Printed Sources and Bibliographies

Burke, J. B. and A. P. *Genealogical and Heraldic History of the Colonial Gentry*, Burke's Peerage, 1970.

Burke's Distinguished Families of America, 1948.

Burke's Landed Gentry of Ireland, 1899, 1904, 1912, 1958.

Downs, R. B. *British Library Resources: A Bibliographical Guide*, Mansell Information Publishing, 1973.

Filby, P. W. *A Select List of Books: American and British Genealogy and Heraldry*, American Library Association, Chicago, 1970.

Goss, C. W. F. *The London Directories 1677–1855*, 1932.

Kaminkow, M. J. *A New Bibliography of British Genealogy*, Magna Carta, Baltimore, 1965.

Kaminkow, M. J. *Genealogical Manuscripts and British Libraries*, Magna Carta, Baltimore, 1967.

Kaminkow, M. J. *Genealogies in the Library of Congress: A Bibliography*, Magna Carta, Baltimore, 1972.

Lodge, J. *Peerage of Ireland*, 1754.

Norton, J. E. *Guide to National and Provincial Directories of England and Wales*, 1956.

Paul, J. B. *The Scots Peerage*, 9 vols., 1904–14.

Schreiner-Yantis, N. *Genealogical Books in Print*, Genealogical Publications, Chicago, 1975.

Walford, E. *County Families of the United Kingdom*, issued annually 1870–1921.

Emigrants

Banks, C. E. *The English Ancestry and Homes of the Pilgrim Fathers*, Genealogical Publications, Chicago, 1962.

Banks, C. E. and Brownell, E. E. *Topographical Dictionary of 2,885 English Emigrants to New England 1620–50*, Genealogical Publications, Chicago, 1974.

Bateson, C. *The Convict Ships 1788–1868*, Brown and Ferguson, 1959.

Coleman, T. *Passage to America*, Hutchinson, 1972. Nineteenth-century emigration.

Cowan, H. I. *British Emigration to British North America: The First Hundred Years*, rev. edn. University of Toronto Press, 1961.

Cresswell, D. *Early New Zealand Families*, 1956.

Dickson, R. J. *Ulster Emigration to Colonial America 1718–75*, Humanities Press, 1966.

Hotten, J. C. *Original Lists of Persons Emigrating to America 1600–1700*, 1874.

Johnson, S. C. *A History of Emigration from the United Kingdom to North America 1763–1912*, 1913.

Jones, E. M. *Roll of the British Settlers in South Africa*, 1969.

Kaminkow, M. and J. *Original List of Emigrants in Bondage from London to the American Colonies 1719–41*, Magna Carta, Baltimore, 1967.

Lancour, H. and Wolfe, R. J. *Bibliography of Ship Passenger Lists 1538–1825: A Guide to Published Lists of Early Immigrants to North America*, New York Public Library, 1969.

Mowle, P. C. *A Genealogical History of Pioneer Families of Australia*, Angus and Robertson, 1969.

Myers, A. C. *Immigration of Irish Quakers into Pennsylvania 1628–1750*, Genealogical Publications, Chicago, 1902, reprinted 1969.

Robson, L. L. *The Convict Settlers of Australia*, Cambridge University Press, 1965.

Rupp, I. D. *A Collection of 30,000 Names of German, Swiss, Dutch, French and Other Immigrants in Pennsylvannia from 1727 to 1776*, Genealogical Publications, Chicago, 1975.

Savage, J. *Genealogical Dictionary of the First Settlers of New England*, 4 vols. Genealogical Publications, Chicago, 1969.

Sherwood, G. F. T. *American Colonists in English Records*, 2 vols. Genealogical Publications, Chicago, 1932–3, reprinted 1969. Early shipping lists.

Stern, M. H. *Americans of Jewish Descent, A Compendium of Genealogy*, Ktav Publishing House, New York, 1960, reprinted 1971. Mainly concerning settlers prior to 1840.

Whittemore, H. *Genealogical Guide to the Early Settlers of America*, 1898. Contains detailed calendar.

Yeo, G. *The British Overseas*, Guildhall Library, 1984.

Trades and Professions: The Services

Barnett, C. *Britain and Her Army 1509–1970*, Allen Lane, 1970.

Dalton, C. *English Army Lists and Commission Registers 1661–1714*, 6 vols., 1892–1904.

Fortesque, J. W. *History of the British Army*, 13 vols. Macmillan, 1899–1930.

Fothergill, G. *The Records of Naval Men*, 1910.

Groene, B. H. *Tracing Your Civil War Ancestor*, Blair, 1977.

Hamilton-Edwards, G. K. S. *In Search of Army Ancestry*, Phillimore, 1977.

Higham, R. (ed.) *British Military History, A Guide to Sources*, Routledge and Kegan Paul, 1972.

Lloyd, C. *The British Seaman, 1200–1860, A Social Survey*, Collins, 1968.

Marshall, J. *Royal Navy Biography*, 6 vols., 1823–30.

National Maritime Museum *Commissioned Sea Officers of the Royal Navy 1660–1815*. 3 vols. Her Majesty's Stationery Office, 1954.

O'Byrne, W. R. *A Naval Biographical Dictionary*, 1849.

Powell, W. H. *List of Officers of the Army of the United States from 1779 to 1900*, Gale Research, Detroit, 1900, reprinted 1967.

Swinson, A. *A Register of the Regiments and Corps of the British Army*, Archive Press, 1972.

Other Trades and Professions

Carr-Saunders, A. M. and Wilson, P. A. *The Professions*, 1933.

Crockford's Clerical Dictionary, Oxford University Press

Foster, J. *Index Ecclesiasticus 1800–1840*.

Gosden, P. H. and J. H. *The Friendly Societies in England 1815–75* Manchester University Press, 1961.

Jacobs, P. M. *Registers of the Universities, Colleges and Schools of Great Britain and Ireland*, Athlone Press, 1964.

Matthias, P. *English Trade Tokens*, Abelard-Schuman, 1962.

Reader, W. J. *Professional Men: The Rise of the Professional Classes in 19th Century England*, Weidenfeld and Nicholson, 1966.

Spear, D. *Bibliography of American Directories Through 1860*, 1961.

Unwin, G. *The Guilds and Companies of London*, 4th edn., Cassell, 1963.

Property and Taxes

Bateman, J. *The Great Landowners of Great Britain and Ireland (1876)*, Leicester University Press, 1971.

Beresford, M. W. *Lay Subsidies and Poll Taxes*, Phillimore, 1963.

Burke, J. (ed.) *Osborn's Concise Law Dictionary*, 6th edn. Sweet and Maxwell, 1976.

Dibben, A. A. *Title Deeds*, Historical Association, 1968.

Garrett, R. E. F. *Chancery and other Legal Proceedings*, Genealogists' Magazine, 1968.

Griffith, R. *General Valuation of Ireland 1844–50*, 1849–58.

Hone, N. J. *The Manor and Manorial Records*, 1925.

Iredale, D. *Discovering your Old House*, Shire Publications, 1977.

Kirkham, E. K. *The Land Records of America and their Genealogical Value*, Deseret Books, 1972.

Ward, W. R. *Administration of the Window and Assessed Taxes 1696–1798*, Phillimore, 1963.

Ward, W. R. *The English Land Tax in the Eighteenth Century*, Oxford University Press, 1953.

Names

Adam, F. *The Clans, Septs and Regiments of the Scottish Highlands*, Johnstone and Bacon, 1960.

Addison, Sir William *Understanding English Surnames*, Batsford, 1978.

Bardsley, C. W. *A Dictionary of English and Welsh Surnames, with Special American Instances*, Genealogical Publications, Chicago, 1968.

Black, G. F. *Surnames of Scotland*, 1946.

Davies, T. R. *A Book of Welsh Names*, Sheppard Press, 1952.

Gardiner, A. *The Theory of Proper Names*, Oxford University Press, 1954.

Geipel, G. *The Viking Legacy*, David and Charles, 1971. Scandinavian names and surnames in Britain.

Guppy, H. B. *Homes of Family Names in Great Britain*, Harrison, 1890. Based on nineteenth-century farmers. Useful for relating surnames to particular areas.

Her Majesty's Stationery Office *Return of Owners of One Acre or More of Land*, 2 vols. HMSO, 1879.

Josling, J. F. *Change of Name*, Oyez Publishing, 1974.

Kaganoff, B. C. *A Dictionary of Jewish Names and their History*, Routledge and Kegan Paul, 1978.

Maclysaght, E. A. E. *The Surnames of Ireland*, Irish University Press, 1969.

Masani, R. P. *Folk Culture Reflected in Names*, 1966.

Matthews, C. M. *English Surnames*, Weidenfeld and Nicolson, 1966.

Phillimore, W. P. W. and Fry, E. A. *Index to Changes of Name 1760–1901*, Phillimore, 1968.

Reaney, P. H. (ed.) *A Dictionary of British Surnames*, Routledge and Kegan Paul, 2nd edn. rev. by R. M. Wilson, 1976.

Reaney, P. H. *The Origin of English Surnames*, Routledge and Kegan Paul, 1967.

Rosenthal, E. *South African Surnames*, Frederick Warne, 1967.

Smith, E. C. *New Dictionary of American Family Names*, Harper and Row, New York, 1973.

Smith, E. C. *Personal Names: A Bibliography*, Gale Research, Detroit, 1967.

Unbegaun, B. O. *Russian Surnames*, Clarendon Press, 1972.

Withycombe, E. G. *The Oxford Dictionary of English Christian Names*, Clarendon Press, 1977.

Woulfe, P. *Irish Names and Surnames*, 1923.

Yonge, C. M. *History of Christian Names*, Gale Research, Detroit, 1967.

Heraldry

Brooke-Little, J. P. *An Heraldic Alphabet*, Macdonald, 1973.

Brooke-Little, J. P. (ed.) *Boutell's Heraldry*, rev. edn., Frederick Warne, 1978.

Dennys, R. O. *The Heraldic Imagination*, Barrie and Jenkins, 1975.

Elvin, C. N. *Dictionary of Heraldry*, 1889, reprinted 1969.

Fairbairn, J. *Fairbairn's Book of Crests of the Families of Great Britain and Ireland*, Prentice Hall, 1968.

Fox-Davies, A. C. *A Complete Guide to Heraldry*, Nelson, 1969.

Fox-Davies, A. C. *Armorial Families*, David and Charles, 1970. Only those arms officially recorded are included.

Godfrey, W. H. and Wagner, A. R. *The College of Arms: A Monograph*, London Survey Committee, 1963.

Innes of Learney, T. *Scots Heraldry*, Oliver and Boyd, 1956.

Low, C. *A Roll of Australian Arms*, 1971.

Papworth, J. W. and Morant, A. W. W. *Papworth's Ordinary of British Armorials*, Tabard Press, 1961. Arms listed A–Z under heraldic charges.

Paul, J. B. *An Ordinary of Arms Contained in the Public Register of All Arms and Bearings in Scotland 1672–1901*, 1969.

Skey, W. *Heraldic Calendar*, 1846. Irish grants of Arms from the time of Edward VI.

Wagner, A. R. *A Catalogue of English Mediaeval Rolls of Arms*, London Society of Antiquaries, 1950.

Wagner, A. R. *Heralds and Ancestors*, British Museum, 1978.

Wagner, A. R. *Heralds of England*, Her Majesty's Stationery Office, 1967.

Wright, C. E. *English Heraldic Manuscripts in the British Museum*, British Museum, 1973.

Zieber, E. *Heraldry in America*, 1895, 1909.

Index